Performing Shakespeare's Tragedies Today

What does it mean to perform Shakespeare's Elizabethan and Jacobean tragedies in the modern theatre? This book brings together the reflections of a number of major classical actors on how these works can most powerfully be realized for today's audiences. Concentrating on the 'great' tragedies – *Hamlet*, *Othello*, *Macbeth* and *King Lear* – the actors offer unique insights into some of the most demanding and rewarding roles in world drama, by showing what it is like to play them on stage. Ten perceptive and articulate performers reflect on their experiences of ten major roles: the Ghost, Gertrude and Hamlet; Iago, Emilia and Othello; Lady Macbeth and Macbeth; Lear's Fool and King Lear. Together, these essays provide a peculiarly intimate set of trade secrets about what techniques, ideas and memories actors may use when approaching tragic roles in Shakespeare's most challenging plays.

MICHAEL DOBSON is Professor of Shakespeare Studies, Birkbeck, University of London, and academic director of the Shakespeare programme at the British–American Drama Academy. He is theatre reviewer for the Cambridge annual *Shakespeare Survey*, and reviews Shakespeare regularly for the *London Review of Books* and BBC radio.

Performing Shakespeare's Tragedies Today

The Actor's Perspective

Edited by

MICHAEL DOBSON

CAMBRIDGE
UNIVERSITY PRESS

CAMBRIDGE UNIVERSITY PRESS
Cambridge, New York, Melbourne, Madrid, Cape Town, Singapore, São Paulo

Cambridge University Press
The Edinburgh Building, Cambridge CB2 2RU, UK

Published in the United States of America by Cambridge University Press, New York

www.cambridge.org
Information on this title: www.cambridge.org/9780521671224

© Cambridge University Press 2006

© Antony Sher: Iago

First published 2006

Printed in the United Kingdom at the University Press, Cambridge

A catalogue record for this publication is available from the British Library

Library of Congress Cataloguing in Publication data

ISBN-13 978-0-521-85509-9 hardback
ISBN-10 0-521-85509-8 hardback

ISBN-13 978-0-521-67122-4 paperback
ISBN-10 0-521-67122-1 paperback

Contents

Illustrations

Editor's preface

This volume has emerged as a by-product of my work over the last six years describing every major Shakespeare revival in England for the Cambridge academic annual *Shakespeare Survey*, where illustrated accounts of each of the productions illuminated here can be found (in volumes 55, 58 and 59 respectively). I have followed *Survey* practice by keying scene and line references to the Oxford edition of Shakespeare (edited by Stanley Wells and Gary Taylor, 1986), though where these productions used different editions I have not altered the wording quoted by the actor. My model throughout has been the *Players of Shakespeare* volumes, the work of which in recording the perceptions and experiences of Shakespearean actors this book seeks to continue, and I would like to acknowledge the good advice and assistance provided at an early stage by the principal editor of that valuable series, Robert Smallwood.

Samuel West's essay on playing Hamlet has been edited into its current shape from the transcript of an interview conducted with him in 2001 by Abigail Rokison, to whom both Sam and I are very grateful.

Introduction

MICHAEL DOBSON

The massive persistence of Shakespearean tragedy as a popular source of live entertainment is surely one of the oddest phenomena in the history of Anglophone culture. Four centuries after their composition, plays often seen as the expressions of a distinctively Renaissance understanding of mortality and its relation to social hierarchy continue to fascinate audiences otherwise long ago seduced by the rival claims of middle-class social realism, of post-modern minimalism or of sheer escapism. In 2004 and early 2005, for example, when nothing else seemed able to fill West End theatres except musicals, the Royal Shakespeare Company (RSC) packed the Albery and the Trafalgar Studios in London with an entire season of Shakespearean death and dismay – an *Othello*, a *Hamlet*, a *Romeo and Juliet*, a *Macbeth*, a *King Lear* – and in 2004 and 2005 the English theatre also saw another major *Othello* (mounted by Cheek by Jowl on a national and international tour that finished at the Riverside Studios in Hammersmith), three more prominent productions of *Hamlet* (one at the Old Vic, one by Yukio Ninagawa at the Barbican, and one by English Touring Theatre), two important stagings of *Macbeth* in Islington alone (one at the Almeida and one at the Arcola), and another world-class *King Lear* (at the Minerva in Chichester). This book brings together the reflections of a number of major contemporary classical actors on what it means to perform Shakespeare's Elizabethan and Jacobean tragedies in the modern theatre, and on how these works can most powerfully be realized there for today's audiences. Concentrating on the plays identified by A. C. Bradley a century ago as the 'great' tragedies – *Hamlet*, *Othello*, *Macbeth* and *King Lear* – it offers the sorts of insights into some of the most demanding and rewarding roles in world drama that can only be obtained by playing them. Ten perceptive and articulate performers reflect on their experiences of ten major roles: the Ghost, Gertrude and Hamlet; Iago, Emilia and Othello; Lady Macbeth and Macbeth; Lear's Fool and King Lear.

These essays are necessarily, and valuably, subjective – recording something of how it felt to these different actors to be rehearsing and playing these parts in the early twenty-first century, and providing a peculiarly intimate set of trade secrets about what techniques, ideas and memories their performances used – but between them they canvass a wide range of our current perspectives on Shakespearean tragedy as a genre. The business of acting necessarily includes the activity of literary criticism – since performers have to read and interpret texts as part and parcel of performing them – and it should not be surprising, despite a long tradition of academic disparagement of the theatrical profession and its claims to intellectual insight, to find that these assorted tragedians have often been consciously engaged in trying out in theatrical practice some of the ideas currently exercising Shakespeare studies in the seminar room.

One of these, almost notoriously, is the extent to which our present-day readings of Shakespeare's plays should be conditioned by a sense of their original historical and cultural context, and the volume begins with three essays on *Hamlet* that together constitute a set-piece debate on how the pastness of Shakespearean tragedy should be negotiated in the present tense of current theatrical performance. Appropriately, the actor most committed to preserving what he sees as the primal, atavistic power of this play, and most convinced that this should involve the theatrical re-creation of the late sixteenth-century mental and spiritual world to which it originally belonged, was cast as the Ghost, the embodiment of a terrifyingly reanimated archaic past. Greg Hicks appeared as Old Hamlet, the Player and the First Gravedigger in Michael Boyd's RSC *Hamlet* in 2004–5, a production which deliberately sought to stage the ideas about *Hamlet* explored by the most celebrated academic exponent of the New Historicism, Stephen Greenblatt, in his book *Hamlet in Purgatory* (2001). One of only two productions among the nine remembered in this volume to have opted for Elizabethan or Jacobean dress, Boyd's *Hamlet* was explicitly interested in matters of religion and the afterlife. Its Hamlet (Toby Stephens) was an athletic, virile, Renaissance prince, whose resistance to his uncle's regime was thwarted at every turn by the efficient apparatus of security and surveillance maintained at Claudius's sumptuously Counter-Reformation Elsinore. In the context of this theocratic court, where the first entrance of Claudius and Gertrude was heralded by a choral Mass, Hamlet's will was in any case comprehensively puzzled by the intervention in his affairs of a Ghost that apparently made its visitations from precisely that Purgatory which his Protestant tutors at Wittenberg would have told him did not exist. Returning in the guise of the Player and then the Gravedigger, Hicks's devastatingly original and traumatic Ghost haunted a production whose simple set – a round acting area, confined at the rear by wooden panelling, with a trapdoor in its centre – seemed to imprison its characters around an inescapable grave. For Hicks, the scenes between Hamlet and his dead father are more akin to Greek drama than to the mundane realism of our own age, giving us emotional access to a fiercer and more religious world, and he writes vividly of his desire not just to resist 'the banality of the modern' in terms of setting (p. 20) but to build his performance as the Ghost from a starting point of expressionism and physicality rather than from personal psychology. Where that expressionism mandates any deviation from the specifics of Shakespeare's text – as in the case of Hicks's reduction of the Ghost's 'complete steel' to a single, outsized, Sisyphean burden of a broadsword – Shakespeare's undead authority must be carefully placated: 'we bought the right not to take those lines about full armour too literally', writes Hicks, '. . . by summing up the meaning of that armour in this one, overwhelming . . . symbolic prop' (p. 21). This was emphatically a bid to recapture an imagined Elizabethan response to ghosts rather than an attempt to translate the convention of the stage spectre into something more contemporary and familiar.

The other two productions of *Hamlet* discussed here took a very different line from Boyd's in terms of setting and design, but for wholly different reasons: as Imogen Stubbs and Samuel West explain, their respective performances, although each was sharply distinguished from Hicks's by being given in modern dress, were informed by two quite distinct understandings of Shakespeare's relations with his own cultural context and with ours. To Stubbs, who played an unconventionally young and pretty Gertrude in Trevor Nunn's production at the Old Vic in 2004, the archaism of the Ghost needed to be smoothed out rather than exploited, and indeed Nunn's Ghost – played by Tom Mannion, who doubled the role of Claudius – wore a modern ceremonial uniform rather than any armour at all. As the double-casting of Mannion may suggest (despite Nunn's insistence that it was motivated by economy as much as by Freudianism), this production was interested above all in the prince's psychology, prepared to treat all the text's Elizabethan conventions (including that of the stage ghost) as so many means towards the end of engaging a contemporary audience emotionally with the story of a particular crisis in a particular family. Hence Nunn silently cut any lines suggesting that Hamlet might be older than a present-day undergraduate, casting a youth to play a youth (Ben Whishaw, a nineteen-year-old fresh from RADA), and the main prop discussed by Stubbs, rather than a symbolism-laden sword, is the series of ever-dwindling heels by which her increasingly alcohol-dependent Gertrude literally diminished in stature during the course of the play. Cast in this predominantly naturalistic production, Stubbs understood her function as an actress to be the plausible enactment of Gertrude's personal story as it might appear in an immediately recognizable present-day social context. Her account of Gertrude, accordingly, cites not Greenblatt and the post-Reformation theological controversy about the afterlife but *Hello!* magazine and the modern media's depictions of Princesses Grace and Diana, charting Stubbs's discovery of Denmark's under-written queen as a 'Yummy Mummy'. To Stubbs, the role of Gertrude exhibits a pampered aristocrat enjoying the new glamour and informality of life as Claudius's consort rather than Old Hamlet's, in between failing adequately to deal with her loved, spoiled and, ultimately, neglected son. Taking an altogether more insouciant view of Shakespeare's authority, Stubbs is prepared to dismiss as instances of authorial failure those passages in the play which do not lend themselves to this form of intimate psychological and social realism. Her hilarious account of her struggles to find an adequate motivation for Gertrude's famous, and famously protracted, account of Ophelia's drowning provide an object lesson in the potential mismatch between Shakespeare and Stanislavsky.

Samuel West, having directed the play himself during the RSC fringe season in summer 2000, played Hamlet in Stephen Pimlott's RSC production of 2001–2, which also used modern dress but with rather different priorities. On a vast, off-white stage traversed by security cameras, West played a Hamlet whose relationships to the characters around him were often less important than his relationship to the audience, the play at times almost becoming what he calls 'a one-man stand-up tragedy routine occasionally interrupted by bits of narrative' (p. 44). Although Pimlott was similarly prepared to overrule Shakespeare's script when it came to the question of Hamlet's age (and was similarly prepared to deprive the Ghost of armour), West regarded this production as motivated primarily by a fidelity to the play. However, it sought primarily to be faithful not to this text's supposed interest in theology or to its dramatization of family life but to its scepticism – about power, about religion, and even about tragedy itself. The modernity of Pimlott's setting – an Elsinore of besuited interns and name-tagged security personnel, which beautifully articulated the play's late Elizabethan politics by reimagining them in contemporary terms – was designed not to familiarize and prioritize the personal relationships within the play, but to show as clearly as possible the pressures towards conformity against which Hamlet defines himself, as his soliloquies and asides guide the audience through the court's depressingly familiar Machiavellian world of doublespeak and spin. For West, the important rehearsal exercises leading up to his performance were not individual but collective, as the whole cast considered the sort of world, both political and mental, which the play's dramatis personae inhabit, and the exact constitutional events which have conspired to shape the ambiguous position of the Prince, who, formerly heir apparent to his father, finds himself at the start of the play as heir apparent to his uncle instead. (Hence, as he describes, they found themselves re-enacting the controversial election of Claudius a matter of days after the controversial election of George Bush Jr.) West's approach to the famous soliloquies, correspondingly, owed less to Stanislavsky than to Brecht. This Hamlet had the authority to stop the whole play in order to discuss whether 'To be, or not to be'; he was able to step completely outside the action to discuss not just his own but the audience's mortality, and his questing consciousness realized at once the occasionally clichéd futility of the tragedy in which he found himself and its ability, nonetheless, to tell urgent truths. Despite what West perceives as both the prince's and the play's lapse into a Calvinistic determinism in the last act, his essay provides a forceful defence of a secular political reading of *Hamlet*. If Hicks sees Shakespeare's tragedy as desirably atavistic, and Stubbs sees it as in need of occasional cosmetic updating to make its supposedly timeless emotional drama accessible, West sees it as proleptically modern, always already new, and hence to be treated in practice as a new play in a slightly unfamiliar idiom rather than a familiar play in an old one.

Touched on in West's discussion of whether an actor playing Hamlet should be exclusively preoccupied with 'personal tragic grief and depth' (p. 43), the question of the centrality or otherwise of characterization to the proper working of Shakespearean tragedy informs all three of this volume's essays on performing in *Othello*. The two productions involved – Greg Doran's for the RSC in the Swan in Stratford and subsequently at the Trafalgar Studios in London, and Declan Donellan's for Cheek by Jowl on world tour – shared a good deal in terms of setting, since both dressed most of their male characters in post-war British army uniforms. (What a godsend to designers working on *Othello* the long-term involvement of British troops in the affairs of Cyprus has been, whatever views may be taken by Greeks, Turks or Cypriots!) They differed profoundly, however, in their overall approach, with Doran's situated in a familiar RSC mode of naturalism-plus-direct-address-to-the-audience (with a set that in the Cyprus scenes erected a high barbed-wire fence across the stage to underline the production's interest in the mind-set of the military), while Donellan's deliberately exploited techniques that looked fresh from the rehearsal room, if not still in it (on a set that consisted solely of five brocade-draped wooden boxes, equally suggestive of ammunition crates or of coffins). Antony Sher, describing his performance as Iago in Doran's production, sees Shakespeare's depiction of this mesmeric villain as primarily an exercise in novelistic characterization, given its force and energy through being placed in a sort of one-sided dialogue with the audience. He follows a well-established line of approach to the role, as much literary as theatrical, that starts from a consideration of Iago's motivation: taking issue with a famous remark by Samuel Taylor Coleridge ('Iago's soliloquy, the motive-hunting of a motiveless malignity – how awful it is!'), Sher finds in Iago a completely full and consistent portrait of a man who is himself obsessively jealous and whose self-destructive project in the play is to draw Othello into the same pathology. For Sher, drawing in rehearsal on the experience of apartheid South Africa (which he shared, from a different side of its central division, with Sello-Maake ka Ncube, Doran's Othello), Iago's racism was comparatively incidental, another reserve of brutality rather than a central fixation. What is perhaps most striking about his essay, however, is his description of watching and implicitly challenging the audience throughout his performance, seeing them view Iago at first with an involuntarily delighted complicity and then with increasing disgust, until in the last moment of the production – as Iago, seated and handcuffed, head down, at the front of the stage, suddenly raised his eyes to meet theirs once again – Sher's reproachful and aghast face silently demanded why they had not intervened to interrupt the fatal chain of events to which Iago had throughout made them privy. It was a disconcertingly metatheatrical moment in what had already been an overpoweringly intense and claustrophobic production.

Sher and Doran's approach to the play was enormously sensitive to its verbal nuances, as this essay shows, but Doran was quite prepared to make one crucial alteration to the text, discussed both by Sher and by this production's Emilia, Amanda Harris. (Harris won, and amply deserved, an Olivier award for her performance in this role.) This was to have Emilia present at the soldiers' celebration in Cyprus (in 2.3), during which she acted as a sort of mistress of ceremonies, helping to pass around the drinks, flirting with the other officers, and participating enthusiastically (under the sad misapprehension that she was doing so with her husband's approval and enjoyment) in a piece of business which became central to the scene, the debagging of the drunken Cassio. Emilia can seem like a minor role in this play compared to the other two, Iago and Othello, discussed in this volume, but Harris's performance was an object lesson in discovering, in the comparatively few appearances and fewer speeches provided by the script (supplemented by this usefully added incident), a playable, nuanced and affecting portrait of a character whose death seems the more tragic for being contingent and incidental. Harris is intelligently conscious, too, of the potential pitfalls of applying Method techniques to Shakespeare, remembering how in a previous production of *Othello*, in which she played Desdemona, one actor complained to the director that 'I have a problem here – my character just wouldn't say this' (p. 72). Her account of making sense of this apparently scarcely written role, particularly of her understanding of the nature of Emilia's changing attitude to her new mistress, and her description of the ways she and Sher discovered of suggesting how the sickness of Emilia and Iago's marriage came to contaminate that of Othello and Desdemona, contrasts strikingly with Imogen Stubbs's experiences as Gertrude: the comparison further suggests, perhaps, how domestic, realist and feminocentric *Othello* is as a tragedy compared to *Hamlet*, where the female roles can seem less important or consistent in their own right than as indices of the male protagonist's state of mind.

Nonso Anozie, who played Othello for Declan Donellan, is equally preoccupied with characterization, though the approach to the role which he describes here is in some ways an unexpected one. Cast as the Moor at the unusually young age of twenty-five (after giving an even more precocious performance as King Lear), Anozie realized, after being bombarded with advice by friends and fellow actors, that his best approach to a part with such an extensive and controversial history of literary and theatrical interpretations was to ignore them altogether and 'approach the play as though it had never been done before, as if it were a new, undiscovered work of Shakespeare' (p. 85). The result was an *Othello* which, from Anozie's own perspective at least, was far less preoccupied with race and with Othello's self-image than some of its earlier forbears on the English stage: as Anozie remarks, 'I am black, so I have, for free, all of those things that white actors had to spend time working on before getting to grips with the story of the play and Othello's relationships with the other characters, and I suspect that this made me a less apparently narcissistic or self-regarding Othello than the anxiously make-up-covered creature offered by some of my white predecessors' (p. 89). What this avoidance of one mainstream tradition of playing Othello freed Anozie for was, quite apart from a performance securely centred on Othello's love for Desdemona, a complete immersion in a rehearsal process so profoundly Stanislavskyan as to be almost structuralist, a rigorous breaking-down of the text into units and binarisms and of scenes into competing objectives that has become one of Declan Donellan's hallmarks. Despite this ruthless process of analysis and definition, Cheek by Jowl's production – which exploited a range of non-naturalistic techniques, such as having characters not nominally present in a scene acting out the incidents or fantasies being described by others – emerges from this account (as it did in performance) as a more fluid one than Doran's, more apt to change from one performance (and venue) to another, and indeed Anozie is noticeably less definitive than Sher when it comes to one important issue in the play's interpretation: according to Anozie, this production's Iago remained an enigma, someone who acted as he did 'for reasons that are never fully revealed' (p. 87).

Approaching the task of playing Lady Macbeth, another part with an intimidatingly rich tradition of theatrical and critical interpretation, in Dominic Cooke's RSC *Macbeth* of 2004, Sian Thomas followed almost exactly the opposite procedure to this, devouring all the relevant literary criticism she could (Coleridge and all), and taking a rather less disciple-like attitude towards her director. Her account of playing Lady Macbeth, as well as being an estimable piece of literary criticism in its own right, provides a case history in the sensitive subject of to whom a performance belongs: was this *Macbeth* Shakespeare's, the cast's or the director's, and if some blend of all of the above, in what ratio? In other words, how thoroughly was Thomas's work as Lady Macbeth solely her own? As her essay gently makes clear, her conception of the role of Lady Macbeth did not at all correspond to that with which her Macbeth arrived in rehearsal, nor did her sense of how the rehearsal process should be structured correspond with that of the production's director. (Dressed in approximately nineteenth-century, Russian-looking clothes late in rehearsals, Thomas had a more tricky relationship still with the costume designer, who originally intended the nightdress in the sleepwalking scene to be distractingly transparent.) In marked contradistinction to Anozie, Thomas, in less easy sympathy with her immediate colleagues, found herself consciously following in the footsteps of a previous player of this role, Sarah Siddons, and her essay provides the sole instance in this volume of a performer avowedly and consciously experimenting with readings and pieces of business known to have been used to good effect in the past. Despite this, hers makes the fullest use in this collection of the familiar modern actor's metaphor by which the performer seeks to identify and inhabit the personal 'journey' supposedly traversed by a character through a play (a notion which, however successfully it may sometimes be applied to the task of making these plays speak today, it is hard to feel Shakespeare can have shared, not least because it draws on a tradition of Protestant spiritual autobiography that would not find full literary expression before the time of John Bunyan). It is perhaps appropriate to this fine performance's context that Thomas's eloquent reading of Lady Macbeth should be centred around the character's unstoppable urge towards a self-realization which she can only accomplish by overcoming her husband's opposition.

Simon Russell Beale played Macbeth at the Almeida theatre in early 2005, in a production directed by John Caird which chose, unlike Cooke's, to minimize any discrepancy between the verbal and the visual language of the show by dressing the characters in Jacobean costumes – mutedly and unshowily Jacobean, to be sure, but Jacobean just the same. Like Thomas, Beale, though just as literary a reader of the text, seeks to vindicate the need felt by performers to ask that much-ridiculed question about how many children Lady Macbeth might have had before the events shown in *Macbeth*: for both players, one of the remarkable distinguishing features of Shakespeare's dramatic writing is his ability to convince us of a reality preceding and exceeding the events shown on stage, of which the play we see appears to offer only a glimpse. The subtle and original reading Beale offers here of the play's text was given expression on stage in one of the slowest, most meditative interpretations of *Macbeth* of recent times, a dimly lit portrait (played on a plain, circular acting area lightly marked with a pentagram and surrounded by foggy footlights, so as to resemble a circular raft adrift in Hell) of an isolated consciousness intently watching its own progress into a world of desolation and meaninglessness. Like Thomas, who played Lady Macbeth in repertory with Gertrude, Beale, whose previous Shakespearean role was Hamlet (also directed by Caird, at the National in 2000), draws illuminating comparisons between Macbeth and Claudius: one of the most distinctive and unusual touches in his Macbeth was the usurper's brief and thwarted desire to cherish Fleance as an heir apparent, just as Claudius at first does Hamlet. This was, as far as I know, an unprecedented way of playing Macbeth's short interview with Banquo in 2.1 (in which Macbeth denies any particular remaining interest in the witches' prophecies but promises to discuss the matter with his colleague at a later date), usually understood simply as an instance of Macbeth hypocritically playing for time, but it is characteristic of this actor's approach that his argument that Macbeth would genuinely like to spare Banquo and Fleance (if he could do so while still retaining the crown) is based above all on a minute examination of the text's verbal details.

For John Normington, cast as the Fool in Bill Alexander's RSC production of *King Lear* in 2004, the business of identifying the character he would embody (alongside Corin Redgrave's Lear, in a production that was one of the highlights of the company's 'Tragedies' season) was less akin to academic literary criticism than it was to criminal investigation, and accordingly he writes his lyrical evocation of the uncanny process by which an actor temporarily intuits and inhabits another self in the manner of Dashiel Hammett. In what turns out to be a remarkably fruitful analogy, the Fool, poignantly and mysteriously absent from the play after the storm scenes, here becomes a missing person, a cold case which Normington must reopen and at least provisionally solve. Normington's quest for the identity of this nameless body – as in any good *film noir* – takes him not only through a whole file of frustratingly sketchy evidence but into some of the darkest corners of his own past (and of Pat Phoenix's too, since Normington's Fool in the event drew heavily on his early memories of repertory theatre and comedy in the North). The process by which Normington's character-ization emerged is here painstakingly recorded, its phases alternating between Method-based work on the text reminiscent of Donellan's, the deployment of personal experience (in particular, memories of a comic called Jimmy Edmundson encountered by the young Norm-ington while he was working at the Palace Theatre in Manchester in *Goldilocks and the Three Bears*), and experimentation with exter-nals. The most important of the latter was a huge cast-off greatcoat, supplemented by a sash parodically overloaded with medals (a detail imitated, in a further instance of the level of detective work Norming-ton was prepared to put in on this case, from an old photograph of the last Tsar's jester, perhaps the last professional court fool of modern or near-modern times). In this garment, which visually echoed the newer, better-fitting military coat worn by Redgrave's Lear, the Fool looked touchingly lost even before his disappearance from the play. Normington's recognition of the temporary and incomplete nature of the actor's work – his sense that there are no final answers to our questions about who Shakespeare's characters are – seems to share the painful awareness of mortality that inevitably comes with these plays.

Normington, even more than Thomas and Beale, is very insistent about the importance of evolving a 'back-story' about the life a Shake-spearean character has lived prior to the events of his or her play, but here his methods of work differ markedly from those of David Warner, who played King Lear in Stephen Pimlott's superb 2005 pro-duction at the Minerva, the 250-seat studio auditorium beside the Chichester Festival Theatre. Warner's matter-of-fact approach to a part sometimes imagined as the sublime, crowning ordeal and glory of any actor's career is that of a master craftsman, rather than that of a literary analyst like Beale or a devout Stanislavskyan like Norm-ington. Trusting *King Lear* absolutely ('Of course it's a great play, but it's a great play because it works, and lends itself to interpreters, not because it is unfathomably vast or impossible', p. 132), the chief priority his essay reveals is not the invention of an entire biography and psychoanalytic case-notes for Lear ('God forbid that I should ever use the term "back-story"', p. 133) but the clear and unpretentious articulation of this play's narrative, structure and ideas. Hence Warner is the sole actor in this volume to discuss where his production placed the interval – or rather, in this case, the intervals – and he talks about exactly how many scenes his character appears in rather than just describing the shape of his personal journey. This heartbreakingly powerful production's overall clarity was achieved, it is true, by a careful and vivid anchoring of the play's every successive detail in a plausible mental and social world, as Warner's essay beautifully illuminates: but, as he makes equally clear, the cast's ideas about who else their characters might otherwise have been were never allowed to distract them from the hard, rewarding work of playing what they actually found in the text. Accordingly, Warner's performance in 4.5, the 'mad' scene with Gloucester, owed nothing to speculations about the childhood roots of Lear's misogyny or research into the real-life symptoms of Alzheimer's disease when exhibited by disturbed senior citizens suffering the after-effects of exposure, and instead his account of playing this difficult passage concentrates entirely on the rhetorical task of making clear the moment-by-moment content of Lear's speeches despite the arbitrary, non-continuous way in which they are structured. It is perhaps appropriate that this volume's cross-section of early twenty-first-century approaches to Shakespearean tragedy, which spans productions whose respective designs placed them in the seventeenth century, the nineteenth, the early twentieth and the present day, should conclude with an account of a performance given in no particular period at all, in a set of costumes that unforcedly and unintrusively mingled robes with lightly defamiliarized modern clothing (in particular, ordinary black leather coats worn inside-out, which may sound distractingly odd but in practice looked helpfully but unspecifically everyday). Pimlott's *King Lear*, like all of these productions at their most effective, was at once of Shakespeare's time and of ours, and productively engaged with both.

Despite the impressive and well-earned pragmatism which divides this last essay from some of the others in this volume, Warner shares with many of the actors represented here – notably Imogen Stubbs and Amanda Harris, who both stress the importance of playing up the moments of comedy within Shakespeare's tragic writing – a strong sense that one key aspect of Shakespearean tragedy is its refusal to insist that tragedy is the only perspective. 'We approached the play as *King Lear*, not as *The Tragedy of King Lear*', writes Warner, 'since after all the characters at the start of the play have no idea anyone is going to wind up dead; whatever else Shakespeare writes, he didn't go in for unmitigated, preordained five-act funerals.' Perhaps it is the open-endedness of these plays, their hospitality over time to a range of possible theatrical approaches even wider than that on display here, that has contributed to the failure of Shakespeare's tragedies to achieve the obsolescence which most histories of their genre (most influentially, George Steiner's *The Death of Tragedy*, 1961) feel should long ago have been their lot in an age which has otherwise abandoned most of the assumptions and practices of Shakespeare's time and culture.

'Open-endedness', however, seems an incongruous term to apply to plays which, however you perform them and with however much incidental comedy along the way, finish with the stage littered in corpses. In the end, after all, tragedy is about death, and one of the most important things that watching these plays still allows us to do is to rehearse safely ourselves for that last curtain, dying vicariously with the protagonists for whom Shakespeare, with the help of skilled actors such as those represented in this volume, engages our sympathies so powerfully. If watching Shakespearean tragedy can thereby give audiences the simultaneously exhilarating and desolating experience of 'dying by attorney' (to borrow a phrase from Rosalind), it can do so only through the ability of classical actors to go on dying on our behalf. (Or even, as in the instance described by Greg Hicks, to go on showing what it might be like to be already dead.) 'Very young performers can often play material which deals with experiences they are too young to have had because their imaginations somehow know about it already', reflects Amanda Harris, 'and it can be like that playing a death: you have never died yourself, but somehow you know this is how it would be' (p. 81). The task of sharing this sort of intuition with audiences, however, can be a curse as well as a blessing. 'Sadly, actresses spend about 50 per cent of their working lives crying, and much of the rest of the time taking their clothes off', comments Imogen Stubbs. 'It is not a great job that way, and furthermore in playing these roles you have to put yourself through the kind of emotions which most people do not experience in real life more than once in five years – which is exhausting' (p. 39). Given the intensity of the experiences that actors have to feign on our behalf in these plays, perhaps it is no wonder that each performer in this volume, while reflecting on a recent role, still seems partly to inhabit it or to be inhabited by it. Greg Hicks speaks terrible monitory truths in vindication of his unforgettable Ghost; Imogen Stubbs declares a wifely loyalty to Trevor Nunn's *Hamlet* and a maternal interest in its protagonist; Samuel West sets Hamlet's narrative aside to tell us his views about the afterlife; Antony Sher lets us into his simmering resentment and hostility towards his senior colleague Coleridge; Amanda Harris invites us to ribald laughter with her when remembering cracking indecently up while rehearsing the death of Emilia; Nonso Anozie narrates his travels as Othello; Sian Thomas compels her stage husband to acknowledge his marital bond; Simon Russell Beale broods eloquently in soliloquy; John Normington tells poignantly funny stories; David Warner magisterially and deliberately divides *King Lear* into three sections. The experts on the performance of Shakespearean tragedy who have composed the essays which follow are, clearly, very deeply committed to their work. Centrally, that work is about providing an emotional release for others, an emotional release different in kind (as many of these actors themselves comment) from that offered by the work of any other playwright. To finish with the words of David Warner, pragmatic and understated to the last: 'when doing Shakespeare my basic priority has always been to make it clear to the audience what is going on. If you do that properly in *King Lear*, they cry. And it's only right that they should.'

Hamlet

1 Greg Hicks as the First Gravedigger, *Hamlet*, 5.1.

The Ghost, the Player and the Gravedigger

GREG HICKS

In the Royal Shakespeare Company's season of tragedies in 2004–5, Greg Hicks played the Ghost, the Player and the Gravedigger in Michael Boyd's *Hamlet* and the title role in Dominic Cooke's *Macbeth*; earlier roles for the RSC include Dr Caius in *The Merry Wives of Windsor* and the title role in *Coriolanus* (for which he won a Critics' Circle Award in 2003), and Brutus in *Julius Caesar* (2001). His extensive work for the National Theatre includes several revivals of classical tragedies, among them *The Bacchae* and the *Oedipus* plays, and he toured the world in John Barton's *Tantalus*. In 2005 he played Marlowe's Tamburlaine in David Farr's production at the Barbican.

S hakespearean tragedy gives actors wonderful opportunities, but it certainly sets them some formidable challenges. When Michael Boyd asked me to play the Ghost in *Hamlet* (and, as it turned out, the First Player and the First Gravedigger as well), I found myself faced with the task of playing someone who had already died and entered the afterlife. Since nobody knows what Purgatory is, or Hell, or Heaven, that would involve somehow bringing onto the stage the terror of that which is beyond our comprehension. However do you play the trauma of being trapped in another dimension?

For a start, you draw on what experience you have of this genre – tragedy – that deals so centrally with death and the beyond, and on whatever physical means you may have at your disposal for enacting the encounter with it. As far as that is concerned, I have had the good fortune to play more Greek tragedy than many contemporary actors. Greek tragedy combines a really strict form (especially if you play it in masks, as I often have) with an absolute chaos of emotion, an internally explosive energy. I think it's very good preparation for when you play Shakespeare, where again there is a conflictual marriage between form and emotional depth that I find very fascinating. I love the Greeks – probably more than I love Shakespeare, as it happens. There's something about Greek plays that takes you closer than any other dramatic form to the presence of divinity – not in a Christian but a metaphysical sense. Man's relationship with the gods is at its closest and most savagely articulate in Greek drama. To me the scenes between Hamlet and his dead father partake of that elemental power: and to play them fully you have to reach beyond your immediate horizons. So as I prepared for an RSC season in which I'd be playing not only the Ghost but also Macbeth, I tried to put my inner psyche into a raw place, and I think I managed that – partly because I'd made some lifestyle changes at the time which had the effect of making me much more volatile and vulnerable, more unpredictable and moodier, darker. (Now it's true that some people would say you need a light heart to play such dark roles – and I'm not at all sure, after the experience of that season, that they aren't right.) I also did lots of physical work: I follow a Brazilian martial art called *capoeira*; I also studied a Japanese dance form called *butoh* (literally, 'dance of darkness'), and additionally did a great deal of yoga. I tried to put myself in a position whereby I would be going deeper than I have gone before. The last Shakespearean role I had played was Coriolanus (in David Farr's RSC production of 2002–3): and though he has feelings buried under that hard, tense, athletic surface, you don't have to open a door into such a dark cavern as you do to play Macbeth or a ghost in Purgatory. So I did try both psychically and physically to put myself into an extreme gear before I'd even started to rehearse.

I took my first specific reference point for playing someone from beyond the grave from *butoh*, which evolved as a direct response to the atomic bombing of Hiroshima and Nagasaki: so I started by working from something violent and expressionistic, rather than something merely psychological. One point of *butoh* is that the dancer is trained to put his body into a critical state, so that the body isn't just acting crisis but actually is in crisis, and each millimetre of movement is critical and quite painful. (As a result I was unusually tired sometimes when this show was in performance, especially when we transferred to the Albery in London and played it night after night instead of in repertory, because the amount of strain on bone and muscle is quite severe.) *Butoh* dancers themselves say that what they are trying to do is to carry within themselves, just behind their navels, the whole trauma of the atomic bomb. I personally felt that my journey into the Ghost was to do with connecting with that level of metaphysical intensity, and I didn't have any time for an interpretation of the Ghost that might instead be mundane or in a minor key. I have seen productions of *Hamlet* in which the Ghost and the prince sit on a bench and just talk, and I knew that wasn't for me. I was interested in Hamlet being terrified beyond the limits of his experience, and I was interested in myself playing the Ghost being terrified beyond normal, human, rational limits too. What I wanted to bring on was a sense of metaphysical extremity completely beyond this life.

But within that extreme state, however you reach or express it, you still have to articulate very clearly the story of a character who once lived and has the problem of telling his story so as to get action: *I need to be remembered, I want my death to be revenged.* So the Ghost presents a double problem: on top of the whole metaphysical question of the other world you inhabit, and the little matter of your being dead, you have to be able to get people involved in your story: *I was sleeping in my orchard, he poured poison in my ear, you should have seen the state my body was in, I did love her once and now she's gone and married him, you have to take revenge for the good of the country!* (to summarize 1.5.23–91). All those statements are almost quotidian, immediately earthly, and practical, and the only thing the Ghost really says about the place he has come from is 'Don't ask any more questions, because if I told you you wouldn't be able to stand it' ('. . . But this eternal blazon must not be / To ears of flesh and blood', 1.5.1–22). What struck me too, looking at the role, was the problem of its now archaic genre: walking ghosts, who physically enter the field of action, are not something to which we nowadays respond strongly. In Elizabethan times the entrance of a ghost into a scene could be taken with enormous seriousness, and would carry enormous import. I remember thinking when I was in Kyd's *The Spanish Tragedy* at the National years ago that audiences in Elizabethan times must have been tremendously alive to a sense of what a ghost could mean, and, to go back to the Greeks, they say that when the *Oresteia* was originally staged at Epidavros women in the audience used to have miscarriages when the Furies came on. We don't have that sort of response any more, which I suppose is good from a gynaecological point of view, but less so for theatre: audiences are liable just to think, 'Oh, it's a ghost.' These days, because we've become more rationalistic and have endured all these intervening centuries of gothic clichés, such things aren't quite so telling and pressing. So you have to try to reorient the audience's response mechanism towards the presence of the supernatural in front of them. (I think we managed that in the *Hamlet*, incidentally, in a way that we didn't in the *Macbeth*.) There are familiar shortcuts – you can signal the supernatural with light, or with sound – but ultimately it's the actor who has to convince you. As I've already remarked, productions where the Ghost is just a man in a suit, just Hamlet's dad, seem to me to surrender to the banality of the modern; I wanted to bring something onto the stage that would lodge in people's psyches beyond the end of the play, a Ghost that isn't just a particular man's father but an archetypal father-energy from a burning beyond which the boy has no equipment to deal with at all.

The practical answers to this multiple problem came remarkably quickly, looking back. Much to Michael Boyd's delight I came in on day two of rehearsal saying I wanted to be completely white, skeletal, sinewy, silently screaming (trying to speak in answer to Horatio in 1.1, for example, but being agonizingly unable to do so), and walking incredibly slowly, destroying normal time boundaries so that my movements would not be part of the living world which was operating around me. That was the first keynote of my performance as the Ghost: being a withered, pallid, tormented, dead thing who was horribly there but also horribly wasn't, wearing only the tattered remnants of cerecloths around my loins. The second keynote was a superhuman-sized sword, dragged with clattering echoes along behind me. This evolved a bit later in the rehearsal process. I came in one day saying that despite my commitment to being an almost naked, half-reanimated corpse I was worried about the text's references to Old Hamlet's martial dress, its stress on the military identity of this ghost – this is, after all, the only spectre in Elizabethan drama who is said to be in full armour (look at 1.1.59–60, and 1.3.199–206). I think it was me who at first suggested that the Ghost might carry a large axe. Michael took this on, but said it should be a sword, and we both agreed that it should be larger than life, Excalibur to the power of ten, and that it should be too heavy for me to carry. Too heavy, that is, except at one explosive moment during the dialogue with Hamlet at which the Ghost briefly regains his imperial and martial power (uttering that awful imperative 'Revenge' at 1.5.25), but then has to let it fall again. So we bought the right not to take those lines about full armour too literally (and to cut some of the reported details, about him wearing his visor up and so on) by summing up the meaning of that armour in this one, overwhelming, symbolic prop. If I wasn't literally armed 'cap-à-pie', I certainly had the 'martial stalk' remarked on by Marcellus (1.1.65). We agreed too that the sword should have an industrial sound, like a chain being dragged along a ratchet. I wanted it to look like Sisyphus trying to roll his stone up the hill, like a terrible posthumous punishment: what this Ghost had to drag behind him was the emblem of what he once was, which he could no longer wield. So here was an intensely physical way of rendering the shock and the pain of being a character who has been murdered. (The one regret I have is that there's one more visual detail we didn't get: I wanted to have smoke shoes on my feet, so that as I walked there would have been billowing black and red smoke. We never managed to do that – but given the physical risks I took as it was, perhaps it's just as well that the risk of catching fire wasn't added to them.)

The major remaining problem, once this overall look and mode for the Ghost had been established visually and physically, was how to marry all this with the speaking of Shakespeare's text. I'd always wanted to see if it was possible to put Shakespeare inside an audial structure that had nothing to do with Shakespeare. I wanted to do it with my Brazilian work in *capoeira*, and we did try a workshop with Cicely Berry, the RSC's voice and verse guru, in the early days of the Tragedies season. It was singularly unsuccessful – we found we couldn't apply Afro-Brazilian rhythms directly to iambic pentameter. However, with the *butoh*, we were more successful. The rhythm of the deep, slow, critical *butoh* movements (and sometimes of the fast ones too) could be put into empathy with the rhythms of Shakespeare's language, and I was able to make the way in which I spoke as the Ghost match the not-in-this-dimension style of my movements, building to a cry of horror in weird slow-motion on 'O horrible, O horrible, most horrible!' (1.5.80), where the rhythm-breaking repetition of the word seemed to freeze the emotion outside time altogether. I was helped audially not only by the rattling of my sword, but by the whole soundscape created as a further context for my voice. The production's composer, John Woolf (helped by the sound designer Andrea Cox) watched me all the way through rehearsal and continuously fed in ambient sounds which he felt would be supportive of what I was doing, particularly a low, burring, oriental drum note that often signalled my entrances. It was a really good collaboration: often I find myself at odds with composers of incidental music (as I certainly was in *Macbeth*), but Woolf was very watchful, and derived the sound off the timbre of my movements, rather than imposing something from a different register.

The other world we were trying to suggest by all this was, explicitly, Purgatory. Following Michael's lead, we pursued over the course of rehearsal the idea that Stephen Greenblatt develops in his book *Hamlet in Purgatory* (2001), namely that this is a Catholic ghost confronting a Protestant prince – so there is an extraordinary dynamic, as a student prince who has been taught that such things simply do not exist suddenly finds that they do. I was presenting him with a world which, as far as he was concerned, shouldn't have existed: his father's ghost would have been bad enough, but I was his father's ghost suffering the horrors of just that Purgatory which all Hamlet's teachers had told him was a discredited fable. That's one reason why I wanted my appearance to be so extreme, so unlike how Hamlet would have imagined his father's spirit if the idea had ever occurred to him: I wanted it to be as if the poor boy had dropped a terrible tab of acid and was in the midst of a bad trip, thinking 'these things should not exist!' The experience that scene, 1.5, should convey is of his mind being bent beyond the limits of his comprehension.

To that extent, the Ghost is a massive visceral shock administered to Hamlet rather than someone with whom he has a relationship. I think the Ghost Shakespeare shows is so much caught up with the trauma of his own death and afterlife that working much in rehearsal on how things might have been between father and son in his lifetime wouldn't really have been appropriate. My only instinctive sense was that Old Hamlet had been a very stern father, and that Hamlet hadn't always met with his approval – so that what I was bringing to bear on Hamlet was not only the present crisis, and a narrative of the present situation, but also a sense that he had always been autocratic in relation to his son. I think this Ghost had always found Hamlet, disappointingly, a bit of a mummy's boy, with some sense that he had run off to university when he should have gone into the army. (Toby Stephens, mind you, didn't play his Hamlet as an introverted weakling – he's a very Outward Bound actor, very strong – but I don't think any son could have lived up to the expectations Old Hamlet projected. In fact, Toby is such a robust physical specimen that you could argue that I'm physically too small and wiry to have been playing his father. I think we decided that Old Hamlet had lost a lot of weight while he was in Purgatory.) Certainly I don't think there can have been many laughs at Elsinore under Old Hamlet. Claudius, for all his murderousness, had probably poured some welcome red wine into what had previously been a pretty strict orange-juice-only sort of court. From what's said in the Gravediggers' scene, 5.1, I imagine Hamlet's relationship with Yorick would have been very important, an escape from the discipline of his father – it would have been such a relief to knock around instead with the local clown. It's very striking that Hamlet remembers Yorick carrying him on his shoulders, and habitually at that, 'a thousand times' (5.1.182) – clearly, this wasn't something his father ever did, and that memory seems like a glimpse of exactly the sort of easy local intimacy prince and king never had. Nor do they achieve it or anything like it in the play; the ghost doesn't come to Hamlet to listen, he comes with one violent imperative, and he isn't going to take 'no' for an answer. Whatever psychic, emotional, intellectual deliberation Hamlet may go in for, the Ghost will ride over it roughshod. That's precisely why he appears to Hamlet a second time, to overrule him: Hamlet hasn't been doing what he was told to do, and has been abusing his mother despite the Ghost's instructions to the contrary, and from the Ghost's perspective that's all there is to it.

So once he has delivered his appalling initial message to his son in 1.4, he doesn't stay to discuss things, and I made his departure as abrupt as I could. At the end of their dialogue, I leaped into an open trapdoor, as if back into my own grave, with a terrible moaning shout of 'Remember me!' (1.5.91). It was a good moment, I think, and it arose from the need to find a way in which, instead of just moving off as if to another part of the castle, I could disappear into another world in front of the audience's eyes. I can't really remember whose idea it was – probably Michael's – but it worked. Initially, we wanted me to fall backwards into the grave, which would have been even more spectacular, but in the event it wasn't to be. It took all my nerve to do it forwards, especially with all the technical problems of how I was to deal with that huge sword while I was falling. We had to invent a contraption to hold the sword's point so that it fell safely in the right way – excitingly, it didn't work in one performance – and this involved my feeling with the sword's point, during the end of my dialogue with Hamlet, and fitting it into a sort of tube. There was a technician in the grave wearing a black glove, who, if I missed the hole, would guide the blade into it – my life was rather in his hands, and we became very good friends.

After this grand exit, for the reappearance in the closet scene I tried to manifest as a lesser version of the ghost the audience meets in the first act, as if I was by now in a lesser Purgatory than the one that I had represented in the first scene, as if something was evolving for me in that other world. So I deliberately didn't bring on the sword: it was as though I had burned off a few sins, so that some of that energy had faded. It was just a reminder – except that this time, and as the central image of this scene, the Ghost actually stood between mother and son. As the production developed, Michael encouraged me to look more and more intently into Gertrude's unseeing eyes (at 'But look, amazement on thy mother sits', 3.4.102), so as to register, even if only for a split-second, a real longing for the wife this ghost–man would never have again. Not that I think that their marriage had been especially close or cosy: Sian Thomas (who played Gertrude) and I did talk about how things might have been between Gertrude and Old Hamlet, and we agreed that it had been a very formal, courtly arrangement. I think they had been the King and his Wife, in roles prescribed by a large, archaic structure: a Royal Family rather than a nuclear one. We even decided that their sex life had probably been scheduled very deliberately: more about dynasty and duty than about personal fulfilment, which is much more what Claudius offers as he restyles the court and redesigns the family.

Having equipped the Ghost with a huge sword and an open grave, it was a comparatively simple matter to start connecting my performance in that role with what I would do as the Player and as the Gravedigger. The Player would also wield a big sword, reminding Hamlet of the Ghost as he raised it when re-enacting Pyrrhus' killing of Priam (and the Player would of course unwittingly re-enact Old Hamlet's murder too, in the play scene); and the Gravedigger, another witness to Hamlet's lost boyhood, would preside over that same trapdoor grave. At first it was a matter of how my having been the Ghost affected the ways in which I played the other two roles, but ultimately they all started to feed into one another. It was really quite peculiar, and, had we run the production for another year, I'm sure I'd have found another twenty little moments that would have made even more sense of the connections between them. There was one moment I loved, for example, that resulted from a happy accident in rehearsal, when during Ophelia's funeral in 5.1 Gertrude dropped her bunch of flowers prematurely – and I as the Gravedigger improvised and stepped forward from the group of onlookers to pick them up and hand them to her, rather slowly, with just a hint of the Ghost's slowness, and she met my eye and was just quickly but definitely shocked, as if reminded of her dead husband. It was in a run-through, and I asked Michael Boyd if we could keep it in, and he was very keen that we should – in fact we started looking for a point at which the Gravedigger could drag his shovel like the Ghost dragged his sword, but we could never find the right one. I think it was a stroke of genius on Michael's part to have those particular three roles played by one actor: they gave a lot to each other, there were useful resonances each time I appeared. He had Meg Fraser, who played Ophelia, double the Second Gravedigger, too, so that it was as if she helped to dig her own grave. These were provocative casting decisions, and the more provocation and inventiveness a production can harness, the better.

Of all the scenes this combination of roles gave me to play, the Player scene, 2.2, was the one I was least comfortable with. What I didn't want to do was make it into a scene about an actorish actor weeping and wailing – though, of course, that's part of what it requires. But I wanted it to be true – as if this actor really meant what he said, rather than just grandly acting a passion – so that when Hamlet then goes on to wonder how this man does what he does, or even why he does it, it would be a different kind of acting that he was talking about. Whether that served the scene (which I was never really clear on) I don't know. Michael kept saying he wanted me to be 'in bits' at the end of the recitation of the sack of Troy (2.2.470–520), and I never was, the way I played it, nor was likely to be. I hope I looked right, at least: the costume was based on my own suggestions, as I wanted something statuesque and contained and precise (rather than messy and slobby), but this may say more about my own anal fixations than about how the play conceives of actors! The difficulty with getting the emotion across that's in the Player's set-piece speech about Priam being killed before Hecuba's eyes, of course, is that it depends on a knowledge of classical culture which lots of people don't have any more. Unless you're playing to an audience who know the Greek canon pretty well, it's hard to make it clear not just that you're upset about this story, but why you're upset. The one thing I felt it did gain from the present moment was a sense that all that anguish about falling walls and towers had some sort of resonance with the shared nightmare of 9/11; the invasion of Iraq was a resonance too; so some contemporary concerns and traumas did smoke through its language, and that I hope helped the audience feel that they weren't just looking at a depiction of a florid actor losing himself in a passion about some forgotten Greek queen.

The whole production, I think, was engaged in that same project – very much bearing the stamp of Michael Boyd's temperament and personality – namely to make as intense an emotional connection as it could with a contemporary audience, without risking that intensity by being obviously topical. It's a strategy which obliges actors to take risks, but that suited me very well. I knew I was going out on a limb by playing the Ghost as I did, because while I realized that the way I played it would satisfy some people's desire to have their expectations deconstructed and the role redefined, I knew too that it would upset some 'purists' – and it did. I was delighted towards the end of the production, though, when I did an interview with Michael Billington (probably the most distinguished and experienced theatre critic working in this country), and he said that after my Ghost the role would never be the same again. I was really quite pleased with that as a result: for good or for bad, I know I was trying something that hadn't been tried before. If you aren't doing that, the chances are you're doing something stale. The Ghost was a venture into the unknown – and so it should be.

2 'Ah, my good lord, what have I seen tonight!' (4.1.4): Imogen Stubbs as Gertrude, desolate after the closet scene.

Gertrude

IMOGEN STUBBS

Imogen Stubbs played Gertrude in Trevor Nunn's production of *Hamlet* at the Old Vic in 2004. After playing a brilliant Cressida while an undergraduate at Oxford and graduating with distinction from RADA, she joined the Royal Shakespeare Company in 1986, where she was cast as the Gaoler's Daughter in *The Two Noble Kinsmen* and the Queen to Jeremy Irons's Richard II: subsequent RSC work included the role of Desdemona in *Othello*. Her extensive film experience includes the roles of Viola in Trevor Nunn's 1996 *Twelfth Night* and Lucy Steele in Ang Lee's *Sense and Sensibility*; on television she has played, among much else, Ursula in *The Rainbow*. Her play *We Happy Few*, a celebration of the 1940s female theatrical troupe the Osiris Players, was staged at the Gielgud Theatre in 2004.

I must admit that I went into rehearsals for Trevor Nunn's 2004 Old Vic production of *Hamlet* not knowing at all what he had in mind for it. I had been a little taken aback when he told me he wanted me to play Gertrude, which isn't exactly the role most women would like their husbands to be picturing them in: I initially thought perhaps he really meant Ophelia, albeit a slightly long-in-the-tooth Ophelia, which incidentally I would not have wanted to play at all (it is a fiendishly difficult part, in our time anyway, as I found even just playing it on an audio recording once, with Simon Russell Beale). From the point of view of *Hamlet* as conventionally seen in the English theatre I am very bad casting as Gertrude: on stage I don't think I even look quite as old as I am, and I am still too young off it to look convincingly like the mother of the sort of experienced classical actor who usually gets the title role. Mind you, I did a workshop not long ago for a director who was trying to cast Ibsen's *A Doll's House*, trying out in my best intense, emotional, girly way for Nora, but instead another director who was there offered me the part of Blanche Dubois in *A Streetcar*

Named Desire (and when I had played Stella so recently, as it seemed anyway!) – a salutary lesson, and one that shows that performers are not always the best judges of their own apparent ages.

I was excited and curious, though, as in a funny way I did not feel I had ever quite got the point of *Hamlet*. Before 2004 I had seen some great actors in *Hamlet* (the likes of Ralph Fiennes, Kenneth Branagh, Derek Jacobi), but the dynamic between Hamlet, his mother, his step-father and his own father had never made sense, in the same way that most grand opera plots do not make plausible sense when the sopranos are much too old and much too fat for anything that is supposed to be happening to them. 'Why are you still so obsessed with your mother?' I have wanted to ask, especially when Gertrude, as so often, has been a dignified empress, talking to a grown-up actor who has suddenly started acting like a little child, as if the closet scene were based on *Psycho*. 'What is the threat? Why is this forty-year-old still obsessed with his sixty-year-old mother getting remarried?' I had not been helped, either, by having often seen the interview between Hamlet and the Ghost – which is terribly important, since so much else in the play has to come from it – played as much too extreme, very shouty and screamy on the ramparts, as if it were supposed to tell you nothing except what a frightening father this man must have been. I know the script mentions armour, but when you have a poor actor thudding and banging about in a clanky breastplate and intoning the Ghost's lines very loudly from under a helmet, particularly if his voice is then amplified with lots of reverb on it, it is so difficult for Old Hamlet to be touched by his son either literally or figuratively that all sense of the emotional content of that scene is lost. It is liable to be inadvertently funny, and, more seriously, to leave the audience not caring, not let into the heart of the play. I knew at least that Trevor would be unlikely to make that mistake, since for him Shakespearean tragedy, like almost everything else – and I've worked with him a lot over the years now – is centrally about the community and the family. The castles and the ghosts and even the politics are secondary to that, incidentals, means to that end. For Trevor the truths that really matter are domestic. There may have been all sorts of ways in which Shakespeare's first audiences might have responded differently to ghosts in armour, but I knew Trevor would be willing to treat them as metaphor, to cut through to the real core of the play, which is its depiction of a particular crisis in a particular family. (Sure enough, our Ghost wore no armour.)

Even though I trusted that our production would look hard for the emotional truth in the play, and even though I regard Trevor as the best reader of Shakespeare's texts, the best teacher–director that there is, my first responses to being cast as Gertrude were fairly negative. When Trevor said 'Gertrude', it was a bit like the shock of being offered Blanche Dubois. (Dear God!) But of course Trevor mollified me by explaining that he did not want a dowager Gertrude, that he thought it would be really exciting to have someone who is still sensuous, who looks young enough to have another child, to be involved in a passionate relationship; someone who looks young enough for Hamlet almost to be in love with her himself in a confusing way. Trevor had directed *Hamlet* once before, when he was about eighteen, in Ipswich, and since then he has seen many more productions of the play than I have, and he, too, has frequently had the same nagging feeling that the story does not make proper sense if the actors are as mature as they generally are when they get to play it. As an actor *manqué*, Trevor had as a young man strongly identified with Hamlet, as so many young men do, and he has really felt ever since that it is at the age when one can see oneself as Hamlet, as a student, that one ought to be playing it – so that is what he wanted to capture when finally directing it again in 2004. So he cast a brilliant young actor straight out of RADA as Hamlet, Ben Whishaw, whose sensibility and even whose looks resemble Trevor's own when he was at that age. In rehearsal, in fact, they were a bit like Hamlet father and son, especially the way Jonathan Pryce played Hamlet in the 1970s when he was possessed by his father's spirit in the ghost scene and ventriloquized his voice. I do not mean to take away from Ben's share of the process (or to suggest he delayed in rehearsal when he should have been getting on with the job!), but he did wonderfully voice Trevor's own very complex engagement with the part. So we had a fully convincing and very talented student Hamlet, and though you can worry about the text's fleeting suggestion that Hamlet is really thirty, or make the argument that in 1599 'student' could mean someone much older, that is not what 'student' generally means now. The role made sense to Trevor primarily as a young student, a modern student, and that was one important reason for making the whole production modern dress.

What Trevor's initial idea of a young and contemporary Gertrude, who would like to think of herself as almost of her student-age son's generation, immediately opened up for me was a vivid idea of a modern social context in which to understand that relationship. Socially speaking, Gertrude could become a Yummy Mummy, by which I mean an exquisitely maintained young mother almost in Princess Diana's social niche: a parent who plays as a friend and almost as a sister to her son but who, because the court provides such unlimited childcare, has only ever done the fun stuff with him, the treats. Nannies have done all the boring side of parenting, the discipline and the domestic labour, and she has just arrived to give him presents and take him on outings and tuck him up at night, only having the good side, the lovely accessory side. I have children myself, and I live in a nice part of London, and suddenly I could recognize that side of the part: that not wanting the son to grow up (I even took Hamlet onto my knee in the closet scene), not being able to deal with all the teenage weirdness, is very true to some women's lives. Gertrude is in this reading almost as much a spoiled child as she has tried to make Hamlet: she just wants to have her sweet little boy again. So at 2.2.69, where she has been discussing whether Hamlet is mad with Claudius and Polonius, then sees him and says, 'But look where sadly the poor wretch comes reading', instead of saying it with an undertone of 'Oh, what a heartbreaking sight, what a terrible crisis this is for us and for him!' I put my head slightly on one side as if to say 'Aaaah!', as if it were much more a matter of 'And here comes my little darling now, and *isn't* he sweet, even if he is having a bit of a tantrum.' Similarly, at the start of the closet scene, when Polonius tells her she is going to have to be tough with him, she eagerly nods and agrees as if with a teacher (at 3.4.7), but once she is alone with Hamlet she relapses and wants to play at their just being friends, as if she thinks she can take him shopping and everything will be all right again. She is appealing as well as potentially infuriating, though, in that very maternal heroism that needs to reassure her child above all else that everything is going to be fine. Over the course of that closet scene he killed Polonius, they shouted at each other, she said he was mad, and he confronted her with Claudius's guilt, but her main impulse was still to hug him and suggest that now he had told her they could put all this behind them, and he was still her little boy, and that was all that mattered – and he left, taking the body of Polonius away like a good boy, as if tidying his room. But as soon as he had gone, she lost it, collapsed, and was just left there, desolate, thinking her son had turned into a nutcase and feeling that she could not bear to think about the awful things he had told her, they were so huge. In the end I found her very touching: the sense of this damaged woman investing her hopes in her son, trying to imagine in a naïve way that their story might still end with the words 'but, despite it all, they all lived happily ever after'.

Hamlet, too, cherishes in his head an idea of the perfect family unit she and Old Hamlet and he were when he was a boy – in fact, this was so central to Trevor's thinking about the play that his original idea for the poster was of a faked-up portrait photograph of Old Hamlet and me looking a decade younger and a little boy as the nine-year-old Hamlet, all smiling at the camera and being everything Hamlet comes into the play having lost. Except perhaps they never were that ideal family, since in Trevor's reading and mine Gertrude had been having an affair with King Hamlet's more fun, racy younger brother for some time before Claudius finally got to the point of committing murder. Certainly the impression you get from meeting the previous husband as a ghost is that he was never a barrel of laughs, all for royal and military duty and the rules, and it is very credible that a young Gertrude might have had more than enough unfulfilled appetite for fun to have indulged in an affair with the more excitingly irresponsible brother. On every level Gertrude has been living a fantasy, a fantasy of being young forever, of being a sexy young thing forever (hence in our production she and Claudius received Rosencrantz and Guildenstern in 2.2 having obviously just come from a tennis coaching session), and when the closet scene breaks that she goes into free fall. She has been pretending you can be sexy and a mother at once, one of those high-maintenance women who want everyone to fall in love with them, including their sons. The Gertrude I played cherished a celebrity-magazine idea of glamour around herself, trying to inhabit a world in which all was smiles, everyone loved her and everyone around her was another perfect accessory to her perfect life – whereas in reality she herself had been the accessory all along.

We signalled this very clearly by the way we played 1.2: expensive, modern, designer evening clothes on the court, especially on me, and Claudius making the first part of the long speech with which the scene begins as a statement to the hordes of reporters and photographers who are there for this official, wedding-day press conference, but who are not allowed to stay for the wedding reception into which the rest of the scene moves after 'Taken to wife' (1.2.14). Gertrude clearly enjoys being famous (though she would hate to be notorious), and Trevor came up with a brilliant touch to illustrate this: she makes a great show of looking coy and slightly but charmingly awkward in front of the cameras, as though she does not like having her picture taken and thinks she is no good at it, and after she and Claudius kiss on 'Taken to wife' she makes a rather kittenishly abashed display of dabbing the lipstick-mark she has made off his face. But as they turn away from the cameras and move upstage together, she is very careful to give the photographers an absolutely perfect photo-opportunity, smiling back at them over her shoulder and holding the perfect pose long enough to be sure they've captured it, clearly loving every minute of their attention. She is used to being a public figure, but is now experiencing, and relishing, a new kind of fame, a new style of celebrity: under Old Hamlet's regime she was just a consort, an adjunct to a rather reticent, dignified, official style of monarchy, but with Claudius's accession the court has suddenly become fun and she can be a centre of attention like Princess Grace or Princess Diana, someone who can give interviews for glossy magazines about the new décor in her private apartments. She and Claudius can have private jokes glancing naughtily at each other during official receptions, and giggling, and disappearing off together, and she can take on Ophelia as a let's-go-shopping-together sort of protégée, delighted to think that she can talk with this teenager as though the age and status differences between them do not matter. There are mothers who are just like that with their sons' first girlfriends, excitedly joining in and thinking how sweet it all is, and that's rather how I played her little chat with Ophelia just before the nunnery scene:

> And for your part, Ophelia, I do wish
> That your good beauties be the happy cause
> Of Hamlet's wildness; so shall I hope your virtues
> Will bring him to his wonted way again,
> To both your honours.

(3.1.39–44)

On 'To both your honours' I indicated my own wedding ring, and it was as if I were offering Ophelia the possibility of a big treat to come – what fun we might have choosing your honeymoon outfits together!

So in a way I trumped the decision to have a non-matronly Gertrude by playing a Gertrude who consciously prided herself on not being matronly, who actually defined herself against the more staid, queenly stereotype this role often becomes.

However exciting and freeing it was to find and develop all this, though, there was still one passage which always caused problems, right through the rehearsal process and the run, and it is in part because of it that I still think that, along with Ophelia, Gertrude is one of the hardest roles in Shakespeare for an actress to play. Very strange, under-written parts, both of them: not a lot there, and much of it apparently inconsistent, and each has one famous big set-piece speech – Ophelia's lament after the nunnery scene, 'O what a noble mind is here o'erthrown' (3.1.153–64), and Gertrude's account of Ophelia's death, 'There is a willow grows aslant a brook...' (4.7.138–55). I think of myself as quite a naturalistic actress, so big set-pieces aren't really my forte anyway, and from the point of view of naturalism, where your task is to find a way of showing why Gertrude suddenly comes out with all this, that speech is psychologically impossible. As is Ophelia's big number too – 'O what a noble mind is here o'erthrown' is about the last thing any young woman would actually want to say after what Hamlet has just said to her.

It is not that Shakespeare is not a writer interested in psychology or brilliant at fathoming it – often when rehearsing his work you come to a speech which articulates perfectly what you would instinctly have said yourself in that situation, just as you do in Chekhov, just as sometimes you do even in Shaw, so that you are suddenly given, yourself, a wonderful eloquence, with the text singing exactly what you want to say. Nor is it that he does not provide fabulous parts, elsewhere, for women. But when Gertrude arrives on the stage in 4.7, to break the news of Ophelia's death to the already bereaved Laertes, there is no way in which you can imagine wanting to do it first with the awful bluntness of 'Your sister's drowned, Laertes', and then with all the pointless elaboration of 'There is a willow grows aslant a brook . . .' It is as though Shakespeare had had a row with someone in his acting company who said they would not play Gertrude unless they got a big speech, and so for a joke he gave them a completely impossible one. The passage begs all sorts of immediate questions, which audiences must have been wanting to ask Gertrude ever since the premiere: what exactly were you doing as you watched all this, why did you not rescue her, could you not have got help? It is clear that even one of Shakespeare's colleagues found it pretty hard to take: when John Fletcher co-wrote *The Two Noble Kinsmen* with Shakespeare later on he made some of the role of the Gaoler's Daughter (which I played for the RSC in 1986) a sort of semi-parody of Ophelia, except that when her would-be fiancé describes seeing her mad and going into a lake garlanded with flowers he very pointedly says, 'I saved her', exactly what Gertrude ought to be able to say but does not.

Even Laertes's responses are pretty awful, too, rather like a terrible bit of television writing: when she first tells him the news he says, 'Drowned? O, where?' You just want to give him the map reference and end the scene right there, instead of having to pretend that he is going to feel better about it if he knows exactly how pretty she looked as she went under. In rehearsal, Trevor's direction was just to speak Gertrude's narration, just say it, not to sound as though I were conscious of it being so very poetical, but that is a very difficult thing to do: the risk is that you will instead give the equally distracting effect that you are deliberately killing the poetry. So you either sound as though you are doing an audition piece, or – as I realized when I listened sometimes to my own attempts not to fall into that trap – as though you are suffering from memory loss, struggling not to be flowery and sounding instead as though you cannot quite recall the lines. This effect was exacerbated by a cut we made – I am all for good cutting, but this one made the rhythm of the passage less fluent, so that even people who did not know the speech might have thought I was just dropping something out by mistake. We cut the digression about 'long purples / That liberal shepherds give a grosser name, / But our cold maids do dead men's fingers call them'. It had to go, really – why ever would she bring that detail in? why would she imagine Laertes needs this bit of mildly obscene botany at a time like this? The speech still baffles me. It does not seem to be aimed at consoling Laertes, though it makes little gestures in that direction; it seems tactless; but in any case it is hard to find a reason why she feels the need to go on and on at such length, in such circumstantial detail. Even then he appears to have missed the whole point: Gertrude at last finishes by saying how Ophelia's sodden clothes dragged her down 'To muddy death', and he has to say, 'Alas, then is she drowned?' It is like a *Monty Python* sketch. 'Drowned, drowned', she replies, as if spelling it out for the very stupid, as if after that whole endless speech he still has not got the message: 'Drowned. *Drowned.*' It is almost funny, and in rehearsal Rory Kinnear and Tom Mannion, our Laertes and Claudius, did sometimes get terrible giggles. Not an easy passage, particularly given the risk of bathos that came with Trevor's desire to take it down, to make it more natural, to stop it from sounding like a thing apart – with which I completely agree, but it really was work, and it continued to be right through the run. I tried it fast, tried it slow, tried killing the tone, tried not doing any downward inflections, and just once or twice I did feel that it was really doing something, that speech, that you could have heard a pin drop in the pauses. In the end it works not for or because of the people in the audience who know it by heart, just as they do 'To be, or not to be', but for those who don't know the play and genuinely are taken aback to hear that Ophelia is dead. But as a performer it is hard to remember that, hard not to come to the words 'There is a willow . . .' and hear a little voice in your head saying, ''Ere we go . . .'

Another thing that makes it such a challenging role to play is how little dialogue Gertrude is given, even in the scenes in which she appears, which means that your literary intelligence – as a Shakespearean actress used to trying to find illuminating new ways of saying familiar lines – does not have much to work on. Instead, Trevor and I found ourselves thinking much more about why Gertrude does not speak more in some of those scenes, with him suggesting that she is not a highly educated woman and perhaps not even blessed with a very sophisticated intelligence, however much instinctive guile she may sometimes display in her management of people around her. Why is she silent, when she is silent? The answers are significantly different, I think, as the play goes along: increasingly she dares not articulate what is going on inside her head, and after a certain point there is an element of knowing, but not knowing, about what Claudius is doing and is planning to do. (I was reminded of Emilia's terrible realization in the last act of *Othello* about what Iago has been doing, what sort of man her husband really is, which comes to her with such force because she recognizes that at some level she has really known this about him all along.) Gertrude diminishes, and Trevor had a very cunning idea for suggesting that: at my first appearance in 1.2 I was wearing four-inch heels, and over the course of the action the heels got progressively lower, so that I looked more and more dwarfed by

Claudius, more dependent on him, and more and more little-girlish, until by the last scene I was in flat soles.

The last scene of *Hamlet* was in some ways as hard to play as the narration of Ophelia's death, because anyone playing Gertrude is again cursed by the fame of the lines, performing to an audience who know what she is going to say next. We did find a very new and immediate context for Gertrude's drinking from the poisoned cup, though, which we had prepared for from scenes earlier. In our production she had been resorting occasionally to alcohol as things got worse: drinking quite heavily in the play scene, and having another stiff drink in the closet scene. In fact her convenient little couplet before Ophelia's mad scene was actually suggested by the presence of a bottle in front of her: 'So full of artless jealousy is guilt, / It spills itself in fearing to be spilt' (4.5.17–20) was spoken with a slight slur which actually fits those almost tongue-twisting lines rather well. So when Claudius called out to her during that interval in the sword fight, 'Gertrude, do not drink!', her response was one of affront, and that blinded her to any sense of why he might actually want to stop her from drinking from that particular vessel. So 'I will, my lord, I pray you pardon me' (5.2.244) really said 'Don't humiliate me by telling the whole court you think I'm an alcoholic! I'll show you!' It gave a nice little motivation to what can otherwise be quite a stagy and awkward passage, when other characters are having asides and the timing of Gertrude's consumption of a whole fatal dose by knocking it back pretty quickly may not otherwise look plausible. It is always chancy, bringing alcohol into a role, because there is a risk that it will look too much like an acting exercise and the glasses will look far too much like props: but the suggestion that this Gertrude might want to take refuge in something that blotted out her mind, if not very original, does make good sense, and it certainly helped me die without resorting to that sentimental reading in which she knows it is poison and just wants to save her child.

I have played a lot of tragedy now, in Shakespeare and beyond: I think people have looked at me and thought, 'Ah, a victim', and given how much I like comedy I sometimes regret this (I want to play Beatrice, someone!). But then again, one of my instincts when playing tragic roles is to find comic moments in them. (That's why the Gaoler's Daughter in *The Two Noble Kinsmen* is such a great part, because she starts off looking as though she is going to be the funny character and it turns out that she is also enormously moving.) There is a terrible risk, especially for actresses, that in tragedy they will do too much crying, and too monotonously, in which case the audience may reach saturation point well before the end. Sadly, actresses spend about 50 per cent of their working lives crying, and much of the rest of the time taking their clothes off. (It is not a great job that way, and furthermore in playing these roles you have to put yourself through the kind of emotions which most people do not experience in real life more than once in five years – which is exhausting.) It takes many actresses a long time to realize that having successfully made themselves cry in a tragic role is not the same thing at all as having acted it well, and regrettably a lot of critics, too, seem inclined to give awards to lachrymose performances, as if the quality of acting could be measured by the pint. (The critics are always liable to go for the easy, big stuff in tragedy – the histrionic men, the barking women – and miss the subtler work and the smaller roles.) The risk is that all the roles in tragedy can have the same trajectory, a countdown towards the moment when the performer sobs a lot and goes a bit loopy and then dies, so the art is in finding the variety in each role, including what may be potentially wry or ludicrous, and finding it anew every time you play it. The minute you have consciously mapped out the emotional journey of a character and think you have it absolutely worked out, and know exactly what your strategy is from one moment to the next, the performance is dead. So the greatest performers I have worked with – I am thinking now of Vanessa Redgrave – are always unpredictable, always convey a sense of it not having happened before, and are ready to relinquish control. Sometimes that goes awry, it is true, but her work touches moments of genius, perceiving the whole play and the whole world anew just for that one audience that one time. Unfortunately, being unpredictable and prepared to rediscover the whole role every night can make it very difficult for the other actors around you! But it is certainly something Ben Whishaw achieved during the run of our *Hamlet*: I found him incredibly exciting to act with, surprising me night after night, as impressive as any performer I have known. So playing those scenes with him, as Gertrude, was, well, as exciting as playing Gertrude is ever likely to be.

3 'Dost thou think Alexander looked o' this fashion i'th' earth?'
(5.1.193–4): Samuel West as Hamlet.

Hamlet

SAMUEL WEST

Samuel West, an experienced director as well as an actor, became Artistic Director of the Crucible Theatre, Sheffield, in 2005. He appeared as Hamlet in Stephen Pimlott's Royal Shakespeare Company production of 2001, having directed the play himself during the preceding year's RSC fringe season while playing the title role in *Richard II*. Other Shakespearean roles have included Octavius (in Sean Mathias's 1998 *Antony and Cleopatra* at the National), Benedick (at the Crucible, 2005), and Prince Hal (with his father Timothy as Falstaff, for English Touring Theatre). At Chichester in 2004 he played the title role in Marlowe's Dr Faustus, and the Master in *The Master and Margarita*. His films have included *Howard's End* and *Notting Hill*.

W hen we began rehearsing our *Hamlet*, in 2001, one of our main starting points was that this was a modern story, and to that extent the fact that it belongs to this ancient genre called Tragedy was almost incidental. Yes, *Hamlet* is very much about mortality, and it is a play which ought to induce grief just as much as it stages and discusses it; but for us it was going to get there by addressing its present-day audience as directly as possible, rather than via a set of sacred, inherited, theatrical ceremonies. The director Stephen Pimlott and I had worked together on a studio production of *Richard II* in the Other Place the previous season, with the same designer, Alison Chitty, and in embarking on *Hamlet* we tried to adapt some of the approaches that had worked on that play for the much larger space of the Royal Shakespeare Theatre. These included the development of an open, almost white acting area within which the action and the text wouldn't be constricted either by illusionist scenery or by message-bearing lumps of abstract set, and the adoption of clothes that didn't tie the play to a set of assumptions about a particular historical period and how that period had conditioned what people could think or say. Despite its stage tradition of elaborate medieval pageantry, *Richard II* had turned out to work remarkably well in a non-specific sort of modern dress, and with what have usually been played as introverted, personal soliloquies addressed outward to an audience who shared the same light as the cast; and it seemed natural to try *Hamlet* from a similar starting point. After all, *Hamlet* was in modern dress when it was first staged – in the last scene, for example, Hamlet and Laertes fight with Renaissance foils, not medieval broadswords – and the play as written really has as little to do with the twelfth-century Denmark of Shakespeare's sources as with, say, ninth-century Guam. So our quasi-presidential Elsinore of besuited courtiers wearing identity badges on their lapels was something we felt we were teasing out of the play itself rather than something we were projecting onto it – we consciously didn't want to follow that familiar RSC pattern of deciding what period you wanted to play your production in and then fitting the play around the décor.

We were also conscious of the risk that, not having the same really intimate and extensive knowledge of 1600 as we did of 2001, we might patronize the period in which *Hamlet* was first set and performed by making generalizations about it. That's not to say we didn't do our homework, but, for instance, if you set your production of *Hamlet* in 1600 you might tend to say, 'Well, it was a very religious age: people believed in God', and stop questioning to what extent different characters in the play really did believe in the God to whom their oaths sometimes appeal, homogenizing the whole cast into matching High Anglicans. The same with the Ghost: I don't think many Elizabethans really believed in ghosts either, and even Hamlet himself doesn't know whether to believe in this one. In a way it is none of Hamlet's or the audience's business whether the ghost is real. It should seem real because it is real to him at the time, but how much that is a result of its actually being real and how much a result of Hamlet wanting it to be real is to be sorted out later. (We chose to make a ghost who could be touched, an oppressively needy vision of Old Hamlet who clung to Hamlet while narrating the murder in 1.5, desperate to be comforted, and people seemed to have neither more nor less trouble accepting the power of that scene with a tangible ghost than they might have done with an intangible one.) It's like that with the entire religious dimension of the play. I'm sure plenty of people doubted the existence of God as much in 1600 as they did in 2001 – certainly Hamlet himself, it seems to me, would do so – and we felt that in not setting the play now we would have been generalizing, artificially narrowing the horizons of what meanings our production might welcome in.

So we decided to set our *Hamlet* as if in a more eloquent version of the same time as that of its audience, and I think it is a tribute to the success of that approach that, right through a run lasting more than a year, in Stratford, Newcastle and London, we all felt that we were performing in a new play. That was the central point: to treat it throughout as a new play. It didn't feel like something written in 400-year-old language, just as, when *Hamlet* was first staged, it wasn't written in 400-year-old language. We were determined to remove all historicist bias, all floppy-shirted romance, to ignore or sidestep all popular conceptions of who or what Hamlet is, what Ophelia is like; all those Millais pictures, all the Gielgud hand-on-head posing, all the Olivier soliloquies-as-voice-overs, and what we were left with was the new play that was done in 1600, still new four hundred years later. It is a modern play, and we played it in modern dress: a play about a man dealing with a society which he finds now.

When you are cast as Hamlet, you inevitably have to make all sorts of decisions about who your Hamlet is as a person, but to me those choices were almost secondary to the decisions we made as a cast about the political world in which that personality had been shaped and within which it operates. You have to do your own Hamlet, and anyone who knows me knows that I don't like what might be called personal theatre, theatre more invested in expressing individual emotion than in addressing public, collective affairs. I don't think Hamlet is necessarily hugely politically minded himself, and of course much of what he has to do is emotional, but I prefer productions that focus on something outside the individual, as being both more useful and more interesting. (That's probably because I'm not very good at acting personal tragic grief and depth, but do have a mind that likes to investigate the consequences of political and social action.) So for me any production of *Hamlet* – and this is something I in part discovered when directing the play myself in the RSC fringe festival at the end of the 2000 season, with Adrian Schiller in the lead – needs to characterize Elsinore strongly, as a creature that (almost without Hamlet's knowledge, I think) circumscribes his action. Despite what Olivier's film claims, *Hamlet* is not 'the story of a man who could not make up his mind'. It is rather, if you want it in one alternative line, the story of a man who talks too much, or thinks too much. But, to expand to a two-line description, it's the story of a man whose conscience cannot bring him to act in the way that the world around him requires him to act, and whose natural mode of expression is forbidden by the way that Elsinore and its representatives expect him to behave. The more that Elsinore is characterized, then the more we can see the pressure to conform with those in positions of power against which the likes of Hamlet and Horatio place themselves, and the more Hamlet has a role for the audience as a guide through the doublespeaking, spinning world of the court in which the play's events take place. Of course, *Hamlet* is almost pathologically self-centred as a play, so focused on and through the consciousness of its protagonist that it almost becomes a one-man stand-up tragedy routine occasionally interrupted by bits of narrative: but you lose an awful lot if you just make it a tragedy of personal domestic foibles, just a sad little story about one particular family in crisis. As I say, I had just directed *Hamlet* when I got cast in the title role, and it's probably just as well that this is one part in which having quite a directorial perspective on the whole play, a set of ideas about what the whole thing is about, can usefully serve the characterization: Hamlet himself is not only caught up in the world of the play, but wants to look beyond it and think about it and discuss it. And shape it, if he can.

We were lucky, if you can call it lucky, that we were working on the shape and feel of our Elsinore at exactly the same moment that another regime was coming rather more conspicuously into being. We started rehearsing exactly two weeks after George Bush Jr was finally confirmed for his first term as president of the United States, after an election which he actually hadn't won: and those events were of course going to be in our minds and those of our audience when Hamlet complained that Claudius had popped in between the election and his hopes (5.2.66). The installation in the US, despite the popular ballot, of what appeared to be a hereditary president certainly provided a useful backdrop to our thinking about the play's Denmark, which is presented in the text – though modern audiences often assume otherwise – as a state in which the eldest son doesn't necessarily inherit the crown, with a constitution similarly hovering between an electoral college and the force of patrilineal privilege. It is important, I think, to do plenty of talking about what has been happening just before the play begins, especially around the 'election' to which Hamlet refers. Our version of these events was that Hamlet had been groomed to inherit the throne, but was away in Wittenberg at the time of his father's death. He comes home, and sees his father lying in state, and he becomes very depressed and goes moping around. He has left Horatio back at college, expecting when he sees him again to be king. Horatio follows him home to see the funeral, but Hamlet doesn't notice him there (see their dialogue at 1.2.167–75): instead he meets Ophelia again, and she talks a lot about his father to him, and they become friends again, and he throws a lot of his need onto her. I think he then becomes extremely moody; kicking at stones, and seeing his father's face in trees. And at this point Claudius – who has chosen the perfect moment to commit the murder, because he knows that it will plunge the country into crisis (he does it at the very moment that Fortinbras is practically at the gates) – calls a cabinet meeting about the succession, and tells them, 'Look, you can either have my young nephew as king as you had planned, though he's clearly pretty hopeless. Or you can have me, a ready, able politician, a safe pair of hands who, unlike Old Hamlet, writes diplomatic letters instead of plunging the country into needless wars.' Hence a majority in that inner circle of electors choose him; and he ratifies his position still further by marrying Gertrude; and there we are at the start of the play, ready for the sentries to wonder about the military build-up and the Ghost to arrive. Actually, if Claudius wasn't a murderer he'd probably be the better candidate: Hamlet, whatever Fortinbras may find it prudent to say (5.2.351–2), would make a hopeless king. But what is extraordinary for people who've never seen *Hamlet* before is how little the play is actually concerned with Hamlet becoming king. I see *Hamlet* as the play that Shakespeare writes when he doesn't have to worry about who should be king, when he has already got the *Richard II–Henry IV–Henry V* sequence out of the way: that is, it's a tragedy, not a history. It's not concerned with settling the succession until the very end, almost as an afterthought: meanwhile it has other things on its mind.

One of them is the sheer sterility of the political expediency in which Claudius and his entourage specialize, its ability to hollow out the everyday world into an endless banal circle of mutual surveillance and conformity, and our production's first important image of this came at the start of 1.2, when the courtiers were lined up in a straight line across the stage in their suits to applaud what was clearly Claudius's first official speech to his cabinet after the coronation. (We reiterated this image at the very end of the play, when the same courtiers, minus those killed along the way, applauded Fortinbras's military takeover just as eagerly, professionally and pragmatically unable to withhold their allegiance from whoever currently held power.) We did a number of exercises around this scene. One of them was almost to enact Claudius's election, questioning each member of the cast to decide which of these people had voted for Claudius, and which for Hamlet, and hence which were applauding all the louder to convince their new president–king of their complete loyalty to him despite their now-relinquished support for Hamlet. (Hamlet had actually lost the election quite narrowly, it turned out, but when you are selecting a king there isn't going to be an oppositional faction tolerated after the result is declared!) We also had everyone decide which courtier had been given which post since Claudius had come to power: which meant that as Hamlet I could look down that smiling line-up, in my deliberately scruffy black hooded top, and know who the arts minister was, who the home affairs minister was, who Polonius's private secretary was, which suit was the PR consultant, and know which had been my friends but had now turned their backs on me. We actually went in for nearly as much practical detail in rendering this one-party administration as *The West Wing* must have done: Laertes, for example, wore a different sort of name tag, as just a temporary visitor rather than a place-holder, while Rosencrantz and Guildenstern would later have their visitors' tags removed in token of their being adopted as permanent residents, conscripted into the regime.

Close to the centre of the play, from this scene onwards, is the cat-and-mouse game – or Mousetrap game, perhaps – between Hamlet and Claudius, in which Claudius is continually trying to recruit new allies around the court (though he fails with Horatio, who watches Claudius for Hamlet instead of vice versa). It's striking that Hamlet can't get at Claudius himself until it's too late, but can kill off his representatives: first Polonius (who, as a politician rather than a military aide, has surely been promoted by Claudius as he would never have been by Old Hamlet), and then Rosencrantz and Guildenstern, and then the co-opted Laertes. The last of the henchmen Claudius puts onto Hamlet's case is Osric, by which time he's scraping the bottom of the barrel, and it's sheer chance that Hamlet doesn't wind up killing him, too. (It's interesting that as the thing begins to collapse around Claudius he becomes less attractive, more concerned with his personal safety, and I think Gertrude begins to fall out of love with him.) It was inevitable, and desirable, that this antagonism should have topical resonances for us and our audience; but it was also important that these shouldn't be forced or over-specific. Larry Lamb's Claudius managed to draw on both President Bush and Tony Blair – in 2001–2, in the build-up to the war in Iraq, people were coming very much to distrust Blair's ingratiating smile, and it was impossible not to visualize it on the line 'one may smile, and smile, and be a villain' (1.4.109) – but his performance was nothing like a composite *Spitting Image* puppet of them. There are some modern dress productions that say, 'We are going to shoe-horn this play into this setting because we think it's exactly like this', or 'We think we can use this play as a very specific allegory about this', but Stephen's production was less easily 'sexy' and therefore more powerful than that. There are clearly no exact parallels for a present-day president–king, and we weren't trying merely to borrow *Hamlet* as a political squib about the Bush–Blair axis; it's just that we were best able to understand the political tensions in *Hamlet* through our own experience of what was happening in 2001. It was obvious, for example, that Claudius's Elsinore would have been fitted with CCTV cameras – just as Hamlet might have turned this weapon back on him by videotaping his responses to the play-within-the-play with a little camcorder of his own (a prop we quite cheekily rooted in the text by using 'O, the recorder. Let me see', 3.2.332, as an aside to Horatio as they inspected the playback). That doesn't seem to me in any way out of court, an instance of illicit 'updating', since by performing the play in the present you are updating it anyway. It is impossible to stage *Hamlet* as it was in 1600 even if you wanted to, because the play has acquired all sorts of resonances since then that it didn't have to Shakespeare, and it goes on acquiring them – during the run, for example, the September 11th attacks took place (giving all sorts of sudden reverberations to the play's massed griefs and cries for vengeance), and the particular courtier played by Hattie Morahan, who was given Horatio's lines insisting that Gertrude should deal with the mad Ophelia (4.5.1–13), briefly turned into a portrait of the Blairite PR adviser Jo Moore when the scandal broke about her remarks concerning the burial of bad news.

The text tells us Hamlet is thirty (at 5.1.140–58), but I played him younger than that: I was thirty-five at the time, but I played him as twenty-five. We chose a very young Ophelia (Kerry Condon, who at nineteen was the youngest Ophelia the RSC had ever had and who, wonderfully, had never read the play before), and I think it's important that Hamlet should be believably so insecure that he might relish the attentions of a girl who hasn't even finished her A-levels. He is definitely still a student, and we much preferred the Folio reading in 1.5 that has him tell Horatio that there are more things in heaven and earth than are dreamt of in 'our' philosophy (1.5.168–9), rather than 'your' philosophy (which is what the quartos say): it makes it clear that Hamlet has been studying philosophy, and it gives you a really good way into 'To be or not to be' by making both that question and his initial method of debating it something left over from the seminar room. If you wanted a prop for that soliloquy, it should be an old exercise book where on one side it's got 'To be' and on the other 'Not to be', and he could be flicking through his old notes, and find those, and suddenly recognize, yes, *that* is the question. He is educated to think around things, to be circumspect, and it visibly doesn't help him bring himself to do the things that are presented to him as his duty. Not that I would say he 'delays': the whole question of 'Why Hamlet Delays' seems to me to be a hang-over from nineteenth-century literary criticism. The idea that you should unquestioningly avenge your father is left over from the time when people unquestioningly went into their father's businesses (admittedly some of us still do, but for the most part people don't), and also from a time when your relationship with your father and the extent to which you did him justice was of prime importance. But even if he does delay, I don't think the reason is very interesting. If you want my opinion, the answer to 'Why does Hamlet delay?' is simply 'because he's that sort of person'. What's more, we like him because he's that sort of person. Imagine the opposite, which is a Hamlet who doesn't delay, who hears that his uncle is a murderer, goes straight to Claudius and kills him. Not only is he a banal character, but he's deeply old-fashioned, a classical revenge figure, and it's a very short play (like that little Arnold Schwarzenegger skit in *The Last Action Hero*: 'You kilt my fadur. Big mistake.' Boom. Finis). The play goes out of its way to show us counter-examples of people who don't delay in similar circumstances. We've got Pyrrhus, we've got Laertes, and we've got Fortinbras. We recognize Hamlet as our man because, unlike them, he wouldn't stab a praying man in the back (and Shakespeare goes out of his way to tell us that by contrast that's exactly what Laertes wants to do, at 4.7.99), and I think if we're honest we don't want him to. The irony of the scene is, of course, that Claudius is not really praying – but not because Shakespeare wants us to think Hamlet should have stabbed him after all, but because the play, despite ultimately succumbing to the predetermined rules of revenge tragedy, shows us a familiar universe in which some things happen, or don't, completely arbitrarily.

The other old chestnut that goes with Hamlet's Delay is of course Hamlet's Oedipus Complex. In the RSC production, we had a less bed-dominated closet scene than many, but not necessarily because the idea of Hamlet's preoccupation with his parents' bed is innately stale or inappropriate. When I had directed the play on the RSC fringe I had a stylised bed on stage in that scene, but I did it in order to have the Ghost rise from the bed, which he did dressed in a sheet, which was thrilling. He just stood up in order to appear, behind Gertrude. I do think Hamlet places his father squarely in that bed, but not because he is suffering from a classic, early twentieth-century Oedipus complex and desires his mother. The problem with that interpretation is that it requires so much that is not in the play to be made explicit. Whereas one thing about Hamlet's feelings going into that scene *is* absolutely explicit, which is that he wants not to have sex with Gertrude but to kill her. His soliloquy before he goes to her room, ''Tis now the very witching hour of night . . .' (3.2.376–89), looks both backward and forward in its comment. He says to the audience and himself, 'Let not ever / The soul of Nero enter this firm bosom' (382–3), meaning 'Don't let me kill my Mum.' Most of Shakespeare's audience would have known that Nero killed his mother, and even a modern audience not up on their Roman emperors understand the internal struggle he is voicing when he says, 'Let me be cruel, not unnatural. / I will speak daggers to her, but use none' (384–5). One can interpret Hamlet's problem in all sorts of ways that are to do with his identification with his father without assuming that he wants to take his father's place in his mother's bed. I think Hamlet's self-image is intimately bound up with his image of his father, and his mother's implicit rejection of his father in remarrying completely screws him up – as would have been perfectly understandable whether pre- or post-Freud. It's striking, I think, that the closet scene is really the only one in the play where there is no audience: this is an intimate conversation between a mother and a son, with no one listening (except Polonius, just briefly!) and for once even the theatre audience are denied any asides or acknowledgements of their presence. The thing about the Oedipal interpretation of that dialogue is that it is, by and large, nonsense, but clearly must have been thrilling in the 1930s and 1940s. I have every sympathy with Laurence Olivier's need for his *Hamlet* to be sexy in some such contemporary way, his desire to find some simple-to-act, previously unknown attitude towards Hamlet that succeeded in leaving people forever afterwards able to say, 'Oh yes, Olivier, that was the Hamlet who wanted sex with his Mum.'

But for me Hamlet doesn't have an Oedipus complex, and, more importantly, he isn't mad either – Tom Stoppard's formulation 'stark raving sane' seems much more to the point. When I didn't know the play very well, I thought, 'I want my Hamlet to be really mad', but as I went on I thought, first of all, 'That's not me' and, secondly, 'It's not him.' I think *Hamlet* plays with something a lot more subtle than mere pathology, and that is the whole question of what a sane person's definition of madness is. Polonius calls Hamlet mad, but should we really take Polonius's view of Hamlet's madness seriously? Ophelia's madness confirms Hamlet's sanity. I think, as Hamlet, it makes absolute sense to kill Polonius and then say, 'OK, I killed him, but you remarried! Who's worse?' In the heat of that moment maybe it would seem sane to more people than just me. There's an obvious appeal to an actor in the idea of genuinely simulating insanity – it's a nice, showy thing to do – but to play Hamlet as a mental patient ignores two things. Firstly, if Hamlet is really mad, you lose the gag of him pretending to be mad, which is one thing the play preserves from its twelfth-century sources and makes good use of. But, more importantly, it allows you to distance yourself from him and to say, 'Well, that couldn't happen to me, because I'm not a looney.' It's much more interesting if Hamlet's first soliloquy, 'O that this too too solid flesh would melt . . .' (1.2.129–59), says, not 'My Dad's dead, my mum's remarried, and I'm losing my marbles as a result', but instead says, 'My Dad's dead, my Mum's remarried, can we talk?'

Obviously, the audience's sense of who Hamlet is and how they are implicated with him depends vitally on the soliloquies, and the way in which we handled them was absolutely central to our approach to the whole play. It seems to me that there are broadly two ways of doing soliloquies. You can talk to yourself, or you can talk to the audience. You are either trying to express a need or resolve a dilemma by talking to the audience who are acknowledged to be there, or you are talking to yourself, or a part of yourself, in a voice loud enough to be heard by an audience that isn't acknowledged to be there. Now, paradoxically, I think that talking straight to the audience is the less false of those options, although it is the most theatrical. If I go on stage and mutter, 'To be . . .', and someone from the stalls says, 'Speak up!', and I say, 'Why?', and they say, 'I can't hear you', and I say, 'I'm talking to myself', and they say, 'Well, talk to yourself in a voice loud enough for me to be able to hear you', I can only get out of that discussion by saying, 'Well, you're not there!' Whereas in our production I went onto the stage with nothing up my sleeve, implicitly saying, 'OK, I'm Sam. I'm not really Hamlet, I'm playing Hamlet, and you're not really watching Elsinore through a keyhole, you're in a theatre and we're putting it on, but it matters anyway.' Treating the soliloquies as direct address to the audience was one way in which we not only averted any sense of there being a permanent invisible safety curtain between the play and the audience, but by which we embraced the crucial idea that the fictiveness of the play doesn't invalidate its truths – without which, why are you bothering with it anyway? This, after all, is one of the play's own points, as we underlined in 3.2 when, on Hamlet's line, 'To hold as 'twere the mirror up to nature', we brought up the house lights, and Hamlet and the players looked hard into the auditorium. 'You're watching us, we're watching you', we suggested in that moment, 'and we're trying to portray your own foibles in order that you can learn from them, and that's why we all go to the theatre. We go to tragedies to watch people doing disastrous things so that we don't have to have disastrous lives.'

It's not just that acknowledging the audience's presence as witnesses seems to be logical, either. It also helps. For example, in 'O, what a rogue and peasant slave am I . . .' (2.2.551–606), there's a point at which I asked the audience, 'Am I a coward?' (572), and there actually was one performance in Stratford when someone bolshy in the balcony replied, quite audibly, 'Yes.' Which was perfect: I could play the next lines, 'Who calls me villain . . . ? Who does me this?' while scanning that part of the house looking for him, and Hamlet's whole point that, 'swounds, he should take it, was actually demonstrated right there, in real time, in genuine dialogue. If I'd been pretending just to be thinking loudly to myself, it would have been dead. Of all the characters in Shakespeare, Hamlet is the one who most needs to meet the audience's eyes and say, 'I'm here, I'm talking to you, I can't go on with the play until I talk to you, properly.' This is truest, I think, in 'To be or not to be . . .' (3.1.58–90), where again we had the house lights up, on my signal at the start of the speech. I'm rather surprised that more people haven't played this particular speech as fully to the audience as I did. One obvious reason for so doing is that 'To be or not to be', so far from sounding like a personal emotional confession, doesn't include the word 'I'. It contains the word 'we' three times, 'us' three times and I think 'his' once, and 'he', but it's mostly concerned with 'us' – all of us, Hamlet, the actor playing Hamlet, every single person watching. If you play that speech for where it comes in the play and for its plot, it is almost incomprehensible: the point of it, and why it is so readily anthologized, removed, transplanted, quoted, is that it doesn't have much to do with what's going on in the story. You could easily cut it. It would be a brave production that did, but you wouldn't lose much. (I've seen one production which cut it, but it was in Russian, so you didn't listen so much.) But Stephen's note to me was 'stop the play'. I came on at 3.2.58 specifically in order to talk to the audience about consciousness and mortality, and although I saw Ophelia as I walked directly downstage, and showed that I'd seen her, what I played was that I couldn't go on with the play until I'd worked out this thing, which is why I stressed the word 'that' in the opening line. It's not about whether to kill Claudius or not, it's about whether to be or not to be. *That* is the question. Never mind the other thing, let's sort this one out. And it's not just my question, it's not just my problem, it's your problem. I could talk to all those theatregoers and say, 'Who would bear the whips and scorns of time?' You wouldn't, but you can't do anything about it because you're all cowards, we all are. We've been given consciousness, and conscience does make cowards of us all. It doesn't help.

It's striking, I think, that in the last movement of the play, after his return from the abortive journey towards England, Hamlet stops talking to the audience like this. I find him harder to deal with after he comes back, not only because he condemns his two school friends to Purgatory if not Hell, but also because he finds the strength to be able to do that by saying that he is God's appointed, that he is acting under orders. And, of course, in the twenty-first century acting under orders has a very sinister echo. It's when Hamlet starts using that argument that we are reminded of the time when he didn't think that he was acting under orders, when he gave himself all that leeway to improvise, whatever the Ghost had commanded. He might swear by the rood, he might ask his mother to repent, but he acts entirely as if the God he has in mind is in his own mind, and therefore his own worth and freedom is up to him. I find him a considerably less impressive character when he comes back from England saying, 'God made me do it', because he stops taking responsibility for his own actions. Of course, if he hadn't stopped taking responsibility for his own actions he probably never would have done anything. But it's also true to say that in Act 5, even though he claims divine inspiration, he only kills Claudius when he knows he is going to die anyway. It's very complicated.

The painter Sickert once said that the only place where God unarguably exists is in the human mind, and I found myself remembering that often while playing what I suppose was one of the more secular Hamlets of recent years. I remember saying to Stephen that I didn't think I could play this text if I had to identify an actual heaven and an actual hell that Hamlet really believed existed. So what I tried to do was to identify the heaven in my head. I tried to make a fight between man's heavenly nature and man's hellish nature, one that went on in a man that was made in the image of God, and at one point I identified it as the two halves of the brain, with thought and with action. I thought that this epitomized the idea of puzzling the will. I could imagine the two halves in conflict in my brain, and that was good enough for me. I saw Hamlet as a creature of the time, who swears by the rood, but, like any intelligent person, has his doubts about whether God really exists. There is one textual justification for this, which is 'The rest is silence' (5.2.310), which for me didn't just mean 'the remainder of this role is non-speaking' but seemed to take up the language of 'To be or not to be', with 'rest' meaning 'sleep', so that my Hamlet went into death saying, 'My end is dreamless.' I take this as an important ending in his circular journey: because he's done what he needs to do he can now die, and there is no afterlife for him, I think, despite Horatio's imagined flights of angels. Hamlet realizes when he looks at Fortinbras that it's just a white tunnel. There isn't a heaven, there isn't a hell, there's just sleep. To me that's appropriate to the whole structure of this extraordinary play, which does a really interesting exploration of the problems of its genre, endlessly postponing its own end, endlessly exploiting our sense that Hamlet is, of course, going to die so as to make him feel more alive than perhaps any other tragic character ever, before it at last latches itself unavoidably to the careering helter-skelter of revenge tragedy and has to plunge to its conclusion. At the end of which, after two hundred lines, there are five corpses, and they're not a very good two hundred lines, and the rest is silence, and that's it. I think *Hamlet* is about what you do on the way to its ending. It's not about the ending itself. Which, if you take a secular view, is true of life too.

Othello

4 'Not out of absolute lust . . .' (2.1.291): Antony Sher as Iago.

Iago

ANTONY SHER

Sir Antony Sher, who played Iago in Gregory Doran's RSC
production of *Othello* in 2004, is an Associate Actor of
the Royal Shakespeare Company, for whom his roles have
included the Fool in *King Lear*, Richard III, Tamburlaine,
Shylock, Malvolio, Tartuffe, Leontes and Macbeth. For the
National Theatre he has played an equally impressive portfolio
of parts, including Stanley Spencer, Titus Andronicus, Primo
Levi, Arturo Ui and Astrov. His films include *Shakespeare in
Love*, *Mrs Brown* and *Shadey*. He has won awards as a novelist
as well as an actor, and is also an important painter. He has
written extensively about his theatre work before, in *The Year of
the King*, in his autobiography *Besides Myself*, and in the *Players of Shakespeare* series, as well as in *Woza Shakespeare!*, co-
written with his civil partner Gregory Doran, which describes
their experiences producing *Titus Andronicus* in South Africa.

I'm angry with Samuel Coleridge. His analysis of Iago as a villain
possessed by 'motiveless malignity' has somehow lodged in the
public consciousness, even though it's complete nonsense. Maybe
it reflects on the psychological perceptions of Coleridge's time, or
maybe he'd just had too much opium that day, but it seems to me
that even a cursory reading of the play reveals abundant motives for
Iago's destruction of Othello. The actor is spoilt for choice. He can
root the character's cruelty in his frustration at not being promoted,
in his racism, in his profound misanthropy ('I never found a man that
knew how to love himself' (1.3.313–14)), or, and this is the one that
drew me powerfully in our production, his sexual jealousy.

Sexual or morbid jealousy is a medical condition which I learned
about while preparing the role of Leontes in *The Winter's Tale*. The
sufferer becomes convinced that his partner is unfaithful to him, and
sets off on a terrible course of vengeance which can lead to extreme
violence and even murder. This is a rare but genuine syndrome which

Shakespeare must have either witnessed at close quarters or experienced himself, for he depicts it in both plays with particular detail and vehemence. In Iago's first soliloquy in 1.3 he says of Othello, 'It is thought abroad that 'twixt my sheets / He's done my office. I know not if it be true, / But I for mere suspicion in that kind, / Will do as if for surety' (379–82). In his next soliloquy he says, 'I do suspect the lusty Moor / Hath leaped into my seat, the thought whereof / Doth, like a poisonous mineral, gnaw my inwards' (2.1.294–6). Later, in this same speech, he adds, 'I fear Cassio with my night-cap too' (306). Here is a man who thinks that his wife Emilia is betraying him not just with Othello, but Cassio too! I am convinced that Iago is in the grip of this mental illness (he refers to it as 'a jealousy so strong / That judgement cannot cure', 300–1), and that the reason he infects Othello with it so efficiently is because he knows it inside out. Again and again in the play, when he talks about jealousy his statements have an autobiographical ring to them. I think even one of the most well-known lines – 'The green-eyed monster, which doth mock / The meat it feeds on' (3.3.170–1) – has a painful personal feel. As does this speech from 4.1:

> Your case is better.
> O 'tis the spite of hell, the fiend's arch-mock,
> To lip a wanton in a secure couch,
> And to suppose her chaste! No, let me know;
> And knowing what I am, I know what she shall be.　　(68–72)

The play is famously about one jealous man – I believe it's about two. It is also famously a domestic tragedy. Yes. And again I would say that we need to see it as about *two* unhappy marriages. The tragedy is that one of these marriages (between Othello and Desdemona) has the potential for being blissful, but is destroyed by something wretched and dysfunctional in the other (between Iago and Emilia). For you could argue that Iago's plot could never have succeeded with such devastating results if it were not for the incriminating 'evidence' of the handkerchief, which is handed to Iago – albeit in innocence – by Emilia.

The Iago–Emilia marriage became critically important, not only to me but also the director (and my partner) Greg Doran. Several months before rehearsals, we held a fortnight's workshop on the play. At the time it was frustrating that of the four principals (Othello, Iago,

Desdemona, Emilia) only Emilia was still uncast. But this turned out to be a godsend. Up until the workshop, we had been discussing Emilia in the conventional way: a little dormouse, downtrodden by her forceful husband, until the very end when she becomes the mouse that roars. But on a closer inspection of the text, and with a clearer sense of both Iago (motivated by sexual jealousy) and of a modern-dress production (circa 1950s but not too specific), a different alternative presented itself. What if we cast an actress who could heighten Iago's fears? A real army wife: someone tough, experienced and sexy, a bit blowsy; someone who could have a laugh with the lads, and drink most of them under the table; someone who might well, late one drunken night, in some remote military outpost, indulge in a little extra-marital activity.

Whereas in *The Winter's Tale* there's no question that Hermione is innocent of Leontes's accusations, it is interesting to consider whether there's any basis for Iago's suspicions about Emilia. Although she denies them to him in 4.2 when she's trying to work out who is corrupting Othello's mind – 'Some such squire he was / That turned your wit the seamy side without / And made you to suspect me with the Moor' (149–51) – in the very next scene, talking to Desdemona, she reveals a rather more relaxed and humorous attitude to adultery. Asked whether she'd ever consider it, Desdemona answers passionately, 'No, by this heavenly light.' To which Emilia retorts, 'Nor I neither by this heavenly light; I might do't as well i'th' dark' (4.3.63–5).

As seasoned soldiers, Iago and Othello know this kind of thing goes on, and maybe have been guilty themselves – with other men's wives. Maybe it's why they're both so susceptible to jealousy . . .

Iago is known as the only character in Shakespeare who lies to the audience in an aside. Meaning his comments about Emilia's infidelity. I think this is as much nonsense as his 'motiveless malignity'. And whether she's actually guilty or not is irrelevant. He *believes* she is. He is not lying.

With Emilia offered to and accepted by Amanda Harris, we had the casting of our dreams, and could now fully investigate the marriage in rehearsals. They seem trapped in a terrible cycle of co-dependency: they're bad for one another, yet are somehow hooked, like addicts, unable to walk away from the source of their torment. There's possibly violence involved as well, with little routines of reward and punishment: 'A good wench', Iago says to Emilia when she proffers the handkerchief, only to reject her sharply the next moment – 'Go, leave me!' (3.3.318–24) – which we emphasized with a rough shove. We looked for every opportunity to flesh out their grim partnership. For example, the polite welcome kiss which Cassio gives Emilia during the arrival at Cyprus froze Iago in his tracks, prompting Cassio to say, 'Let it not gall your patience, good Iago, / That I extend my manners' (2.1.100–1). We also put Emilia into a sequence where she doesn't normally appear – the drinking binge in 2.3 – and this facilitated more moments between her and Iago: her arrival with the revellers, which surprised him and which he then 'allowed'; her drunken participation in the debagging of Cassio during the King Stephen song, which shocked Iago senseless – *here, before his very eyes, was proof of her intimacy with Cassio!* – and her exit from the scene, when she flirtatiously tried to take Iago away to bed and was viciously rejected. But Iago's truest feelings about his wife come out in his choice of words at the end, when she reveals the truth about the handkerchief – he calls her 'villainous whore' and 'filth' (5.2.236, 238). We had him kill her with a frenzied stabbing between her legs.

I've discussed the Iago–Emilia relationship first and at length, because I regard it as key to Iago's motivation, but of course his main relationship in the story is that with his superior officer and, apparently, his friend, Othello. Of the play's three thousand lines they share an amazing two thousand between them, and large passages of the play – like the huge Jealousy Scene, 3.3 – are just two-handers. (For the collector of statistics, it's also worth mentioning that Iago is the third biggest part in Shakespeare, after Hamlet and Richard III.)

Greg and I had been talking about doing *Othello* for many, many years, but could never think of the right person for the title role. Then in 1995 we did a production of *Titus Andronicus* at the renowned Market Theatre in Johannesburg, and were lucky enough to get one of South Africa's top actors, Sello-Maake ka Ncube, to play Aaron the Moor. (Aaron is Shakespeare's other great black role, although ironically it's more an early sketch for Iago than Othello.) We said then, 'When we finally do *Othello* he's the man to play it.' Sello possesses all the qualities that an Othello needs: a natural nobility, it's a kind of spiritual grace, as well as enormous gentleness and vulnerability – qualities which allow him to be both madly in love and madly jealous – and finally, and perhaps most importantly, formidable danger. When Othello blows, he blows. We're talking volcanoes or earthquakes: an unstoppable force of nature. Some black commentators say that the play is racist because Othello, once roused, reverts to being a violent savage. But this is to deny one of Shakespeare's most searing observations about human behaviour – when we're under extreme pressure, the animal in us takes over. Call it savage, call it primal, call it what you will, but it manifests itself in Lear, Titus, Shylock, Leontes . . . the list is long, and they're not black.

Almost ten years after *Titus Andronicus*, our wish came true, and we were able to do *Othello* with the actor we wanted. Sello ended up giving a remarkable performance: the part flowed through him as naturally as blood or breath, driven by a special, unmistakable African power.

The fact that Sello and I are both South African was an almost incidental factor, but it became an enormous plus. Brought up on either side of the apartheid boundary, which stood like a Berlin Wall in the South Africa of our youth – built not of solid concrete but crazy ideology – we were able to bring a lot of first-hand experience to the racism in the play. This racism is an important theme, I think, though not the primary one. Venice is undeniably a racist society. Some of Brabantio's language shocks even a hardened white South African like me. In playing Iago's racism, I drew on the attitudes of the ruling Nationalist Party in the old South Africa, and their staunchest supporters, the Afrikaners. Blacks were not so much despised by them as disregarded – they were second-class citizens, an inferior form of human life. An Afrikaner wouldn't expend the energy of hatred on black people; his feelings were more likely to be expressed as mockery. Blacks were stupid and clumsy, they were clowns, they were apes. So in 1.1 when Iago quotes Othello – '"For Certes" says he, / "I have already chose my officer"' (15–16) – I imitated a gorilla's walk and spoke in a cod African accent. An even richer opportunity presented itself in 4.1 when Othello collapses with the epileptic fit. This is one of the supreme moments of triumph for Iago. His victim lies unconscious at his feet. The actor playing Iago has a range of choices here. How to express his feelings? For me it was very simple. Earlier, in 3.3, when Sello said the line, 'Arise black vengeance from thy hollow cell' (451), he went into a form of Zulu war-dancing, with dynamic stamps and swooping gestures round his head. So now, when he was struck down by epilepsy, I did a grotesque mimicry of the war-dance, ending astride him and beating my chest, ape-like again.

Iago sneers at Othello for being black, but his contempt extends to everyone else in the play, and to humanity in general. The line I quoted earlier – 'I never found a man that knew how to love himself' – is an exceptionally bleak statement: it pictures a world of self-doubting, self-hating people. Does this miserable population include Iago himself? In 5.1, he says a strange thing when talking about Cassio: 'He hath a daily beauty in his life / That makes me ugly' (19–20). This is an extraordinary confession – that another person's beauty, physical or inner, should reflect negatively on your own sense of self – and could only come from somebody riddled with jealousy and inner loathing.

In his excellent essay on the play, W. H. Auden wrote that 'Since the ultimate goal of Iago is nothingness, he must not only destroy others, but himself as well.' I found this inspiring. After all, there is no practical gain in destroying Othello and the others; there's no financial, professional or sexual advantage to be won; Iago just seems to be on some nihilistic joy-ride. This notion led to me playing the couplet at the end of 5.1 – 'This is the night / That either makes me or fordoes me quite' (130–1) – as offering a buzz either way. And in the final scene, when Othello wounds Iago, I played the line, 'I bleed sir, but not killed' (5.2.294), with a note of disappointment, as though deprived of the next helter-skelter jaunt – into the underworld.

Auden also talks of Iago as a kind of scientist, experimenting with human nature. Greg and I sought every opportunity to reveal this. It's probably most explicit in the speech in the middle of 3.3, when Iago himself seems amazed by the speed of his effect on Othello:

> The Moor already changes with my poison.
> Dangerous conceits are in their natures poisons,
> Which at the first are scarce found to distaste,
> But with a little act upon the blood,
> Burn like the mines of sulphur. (329–33)

Using a clinical and objective tone whenever possible in Iago's speeches helps to avoid the major pitfall of the role: playing him as a stage villain, with pantomime relish, and one eye constantly winking at the audience. The American actor James Earl Jones, who played Othello seven times, has written angrily about the experience of doing it with Christopher Plummer, who so exploited the comic potential of Iago that he transformed The Tragedy of Othello into 'a bloody farce'. This is easily done. Iago's methods are so daring and outrageous that the audience are often tempted to laugh. The *right* kind of laughter, which is nervy, almost closer to gasping, is apt and useful: it increases the tension, and can be cut off abruptly to create an electric silence. The *wrong* kind of laughter, however – and I did everything in my power to kill this – will hijack the entire story: Othello simply becomes a fool, a dupe, and there's nothing more to it.

We're now onto something at the very heart of the play, and which certain people regard as its fatal flaw, while others, like myself, hold it as one of its greatest assets: Othello's apparent gullibility. Is he abnormally naïve and credulous? I don't think so. Although he certainly has a 'free and open nature' – Iago identifies this as part of his character – it's not a dishonourable quality, it's not a fault; if anything it contributes to his charm and charisma at the beginning. No, I think we could all be Othellos. We could all be deceived by the right lies. And after all, Othello is not the fall guy of some third-rate con-man. Iago is a master of his craft. I think of him as a master torturer. He is able to play both the good cop and the bad cop at the same time. At the start of the big Jealousy Scene, he implores Othello not to question him further: 'It were not for your quiet nor your good / . . . / To let you know my thoughts' (3.3.157–9). He uses *truth* as a weapon. He urges Othello to doubt his words: 'Say they are vile and false?' (141). Later in the scene, he says, 'Let me be thought too busy in my fears, / As worthy cause I have to fear I am' (258–9). All this is *true*. In a curious way, he is being 'honest Iago'. Except, of course, the more he tells Othello not to pursue the matter, the more it fuels Othello's curiosity and disquiet. These are brilliant tactics.

I wonder if 3.3 is not the greatest single scene in all of Shakespeare. It's like a gruesome but thrilling boxing match, with two prize fighters slugging it out. In playing time, it lasts half an hour. That fateful period begins with Othello blissfully in love with his new bride, and ends with him resolving to murder her. In between, Iago has performed an exercise of psychological torture which shocks you senseless, yet takes your breath away. The scene was tiring to perform, yet every time I exited from it, I felt exhilarated too, dazzled by Shakespeare's genius.

This also shows itself in Iago's use of the audience. They are, along with Othello, Desdemona, Emilia and Roderigo, one of Iago's chief victims. They are complicit with him – he forces them to be, by confiding in them. He is the torturer who takes you by the hand and invites you sit in the corner while he works. And, surprisingly, the audience become strangely attracted to the process. When I spoke the soliloquies, I was intrigued by a distinctive expression I saw on faces in the front few rows: a peculiar smile, a peculiar kind of excitement. In listening to me, in sharing my dangerous secrets, they were doing something very immoral, very naughty, and they *liked* it. By the end, however, their empathy had entirely switched to Othello, Desdemona and Emilia, and now their feelings were of horror and grief. I received several letters from people who said they felt soiled by the journey. Throughout the run, I waited for the performance when someone would stand up and shout, 'Stop it!'

When Greg directs Shakespeare, one of his passions is to look for what he calls 'crossroads'. Because the stories of these classic plays are so familiar, almost over-familiar, he believes you have to find ways to make the audience think that things might go differently this time. You do this by playing critical moments with complete spontaneity, openness and lack of premeditation. Which is, after all, only what happens in our daily lives; no one has rehearsed us, no one has shown us the script; we are all improvisers.

With Iago, Greg's special insight was to encourage me to view him as the Great Improviser. On a first reading of the play, Iago seems to be totally in control, like some omniscient puppeteer. He tells us what's going to happen, and then makes it come true. You could play him like this, but it's not very interesting, for the events lose tension. So what if Iago doesn't know what the next scene holds? What if he's having to think on his feet, risking exposure with every step? For this particular puppeteer needs to be very careful: his puppets are living, breathing people; they might talk to one another at the wrong moment, reveal the wrong thing, they might see what the others are doing, and issues of guilt or innocence might suddenly be out in the open. Greg maintained that at the beginning Iago can't possibly dream of achieving the sheer amount of chaos which ensues, culminating in the death of *four* people. Instead, he proceeds step by step, trying this, trying that, testing out his methods of manipulation on a couple of small-fries, Roderigo and Cassio, before taking on the main man. A good example of the Great Improviser at work occurs in the Jealousy Scene when Othello demands: 'Give me a living reason she's disloyal' (3.3.414).

Iago obviously can't answer that. So instead he invents the weird tale of sharing a bed with Cassio, and being on the receiving end of what is virtually a wet dream about Desdemona. Another improvisation, and a perilous one, is the eavesdropping sequence in 4.1, when Iago contrives to question Cassio about Bianca, getting him to mock and demean her, while Othello listens, thinking that the conversation is about Desdemona. One wrong word here, and the entire plot would be blown open.

Greg constantly urged me to find moments where Iago is surprised by developments, excited or confounded by them. Never more so than when Desdemona seeks his help in 4.2. In our production, Desdemona (played by the remarkable newcomer Lisa Dillon) broke down and hugged Iago, making him rock her. For me, this was the most dangerous moment in the whole play. Here in my arms was the beautiful woman I both desired and despised, and whose murder I was planning. The audience was aghast, on the verge of nervous laughter. Could this be happening? I shared their amazement. On the one hand, it was confusing, this simple human embrace (Iago doesn't have much experience of such things); on the other hand, it was sexually exciting beyond belief, and when I stood up I quickly adjusted my clothing.

This was also a dynamic 'crossroads' moment. When Desdemona was in my arms, we played it so tenderly the audience could be forgiven for hoping that Iago was about to relent and abort the plan.

Another 'crossroads' occured when Othello was struck down by the epileptic fit, and Iago was doing his mimicry of the Zulu war-dance. Greg advanced Cassio's entrance by a few beats, giving Iago a terrible fright (*did Cassio see?*), and this fright was then intensified as Othello recovered and immediately asked Iago, 'Dost thou mock me?' I played Iago speechless for a long moment (*did Othello see?*), and then covered up with aggression: 'I mock you? No by heaven! / Would you would bear your fortune like a man!' (4.1.58–9). And so we sought every opportunity to almost trip up Iago. Unless he's walking a tightrope, everything becomes too easy. The play is about human frailty, and this should include Iago. He is much more fascinating as a human being than as a devil.

His sexuality is worth an essay in itself. He doesn't seem to be able to open his mouth without talking about sex, and it is often with the slavering prurience of a tabloid journalist, filled with lust and disgust at the same time. (This is, incidentally, a quality which Iago shares with Leontes.) When Iago is trying to convince Roderigo that Desdemona and Cassio fancy one another, he says that Cassio is 'a pestilent complete knave, and the woman hath found him already' (2.1.247–8). This is a typical piece of Iago sex imagery, visceral and sick: Cassio depicted as a piece of diseased flesh, whose sweet stench is attracting scavengers. To Iago, sex seems to be a foul appetite, something you devour. 'The food that to him now is as luscious as locusts', he says of Othello and Desdemona, 'shall be to him shortly as acerbic as the coloquintida' (1.3.347–8). (Even of kissing he says: 'he plucked up kisses by the roots / That grew upon my lips' (3.3.427–8).) Or else sex is just brutish: it is just 'making the beast with two backs' (1.1.118–19). Animals crop up a lot in his dirty talk. He says to Brabantio, 'an old black ram / Is tupping your white ewe', and 'you'll have your daughter covered with a Barbary horse' (88–9, 113–14). And later, he taunts Othello with these pictures: 'It is impossible you should see this, / Were they as prime as goats, as hot as monkeys, / As salt as wolves in pride' (3.3.408–9). According to Iago, sex is a savage business of gorging and rutting; there's certainly nothing loving about it.

Although he talks about sex all the time, you don't get the feeling he does much of it himself. So what's going on – is he impotent, is he a closet gay? Long before his success in the title role, Olivier played Iago, and he was drawn to the gay notion. At one rehearsal of the epilepsy sequence, he tried kissing the unconscious Othello – the improbably cast Ralph Richardson – only to be rebuffed with the immortal line, 'Steady on, old boy', which curtailed any further exploration of the idea. Later, when Frank Finlay played Iago to Olivier's Moor, he favoured the impotent theory. I'm not entirely sure what this is based on. Perhaps the moment when Iago confesses to the audience that he loves Desdemona, and then adds, with strange defensiveness: 'Not out of absolute lust – though peradventure / I stand accountant for as great a sin' (2.1.291–2). Anyway, I'm not persuaded by either of these proposals. I hate the idea of Iago's 'villainy' stemming from any kind of gayness, and I feel that certain moments of the action do arouse him strongly: the embrace with Desdemona in our production, and also the sight of her dead body. I think that when it comes to sex, as in all other matters, Iago is just thoroughly perverse and individualistic. A clue comes in the crucial moment when Emilia decides to steal Desdemona's handkerchief and give it to Iago. She says, 'What he will do with it, heaven knows, not I / I nothing, but to please his fantasy' (3.3.301–3). Perhaps the Great Improviser is also the Great Masturbator.

Along with a constant undertow of sexual imagery, Shakespeare peppers Iago's language with another distinctive trait: the cryptic comment. This is established straight away in 1.1, when he says, 'For sir, / It is as sure as you are Roderigo, / Were I the Moor, I would not be Iago' (56–7). Another example is in the big 3.3 temptation, when he says to Othello, 'Men should be what they seem; / Or those that be not, would they might seem none' (131–2). In 4.1, after Othello has slapped Desdemona, Lodovico asks what's happened to the noble Moor, and Iago answers, 'He's that he is. I may not breathe my censure / What he might be. If what he might he is not, / I would to heaven he were' (272–4). And even in his final speech, in 5.2, he says, 'What you know, you know' (309). I liked these cryptic comments very much, and in performance emphasized them with a little sing-song rhythm. I think they help to reveal Iago's sense of superiority and mischief (Auden describes him as a practical joker as well as a scientist), in that he sometimes talks to people using a kind of code which they can't necessarily understand. I also wonder if it's not a defence mechanism. 'You may relish him more in the soldier than in the scholar', Cassio says of Iago (2.1.168–9). Patronizing perhaps, but true. Although Iago has natural cunning, which allows him to think faster than anyone else, he is not an intellectual. Perhaps, in order to cover up, he tries to sound cleverer than he is.

Iago's military identity became vital to my view of the role. His rank is obviously important to the plot. We chose to call him 'Ensign' rather than 'Ancient', and, in our modern-dress context, decided this was equivalent to being an RSM. I played him as a non-commissioned officer down to the soles of his square-bashing boots, and regarded his expectation of promotion to lieutenant as sheer fantasy. (Even though he unexpectedly achieves this at the end of the Jealousy Scene.) But I believe his military identity isn't just a professional matter; it also profoundly affects the inner man.

When I was growing up in South Africa, there was compulsory conscription for the white population, and so I did my stint of army service. I remember being both fascinated and terrified by the process at hand. We were being broken down as individuals only to be built up as soldiers: a mass of people who operate as though life had only two brutal principles – power and violence. You get orders and you carry them out. Whenever this system produces atrocities – Auschwitz, My Lai, Sharpeville, Abu Ghraib, etcetera – we throw up our hands in horror and ask who are these evil people? Well, they're just us – broken down and built up by the military. I think that Iago, who is a career soldier through and through (he talks of 'the trade of war', 1.2.1), only goes a few steps further than his comrades. His disregard for human feelings, even human life, is rooted in his training. In our production we did everything possible to put Iago in context. By showing his popularity with the soldiers – they greatly enjoyed his suggestive banter during the arrival at Cyprus, and his wild drinking party later that night – and by showing their own inherent cruelty: their gleeful participation in getting Cassio drunk, and their preparations to interrogate/rape Bianca in 5.1.

The role of Iago is almost totally schizophrenic. It nearly breaks down into two neat halves; the private man (i.e. the soliloquies, which reveal all his plans and all his demons) and the public man (generally perceived as 'honest Iago'), and I played these two personalities as markedly different: in private he was driven, bitter, feverish with jealousy, quite unstable, while in public he was relaxed, reassuring, entertaining, efficient. But there is one grey area in between the two: the Roderigo scenes. In these, Iago shows both sides of his persona, now outlining his devious plans, now being the reliable friend. Roderigo himself is a unique character in the play. Apart from a brief exchange with Brabantio, and two violent attacks on Cassio, he never talks to anyone other than Iago, and even here is mostly drowned out by his garrulous companion. Roderigo can be a rather bland stage presence – just a sounding-board for Iago, just the man who pays the bills, just another dupe – but we were fortunate to have Mark Lockyer in the role, playing him as an angry and neurotic misfit, obsessively in love with Desdemona, deeply mistrustful of Iago, forever trying *not* to be exploited. This gave our scenes together a terrific tension, and added fuel to Greg's notion that Iago could be caught out at any moment. In 4.2, immediately after Iago has comforted Desdemona, we had him return to her room to rifle through her portmanteau, sniffing and fondling her clothes – and then Roderigo suddenly entered, almost discovering him at it. In the ensuing showdown, when Roderigo demands to know what's happened to the jewels he's given Iago for Desdemona, he threatens: 'I will make myself known to

Desdemona' (4.2.201–2). Well, if only he *did*, the whole tragedy would be averted.

The Roderigo scenes also provide Shakespeare with further chances to explore that ultimate stroke of *chutzpah* in the writing of Iago: his unexpected tendency to tell the truth. In their first scene together, Iago tells Roderigo, 'when my outward action doth demonstrate / The native act and figure of my heart / In compliment extern, 'tis not long after / But I will wear my heart upon my sleeve / For daws to peck at'. This doesn't arouse suspicion in Roderigo, but rather trust – he's flattered to be the confidant of this intriguing anarchist. No alarm bells ring even when Iago imparts the starkest of facts: 'I am not what I am' (1.1.61–5).

I think Iago is one of most mesmeric and original characters in all of drama. A disturbed and disturbing man, who, despite his cruelty and amorality, attracts us powerfully. And look at the extraordinary ending which Shakespeare gives him. Captured and wounded, facing torture and interrogation, his last line is: 'From this time forth, I never will speak word' (5.2.310). This from the third wordiest part in the canon, this from the man who has used torrents of words to seduce and trick all the other characters in the play, as well as the audience. The Great Improviser has once again found the most unexpected solution to his present situation: silence.

In our production, Iago was left in a sitting position after Othello wounded him; hand-cuffed, head bowed. Then after Lodovico's closing couplet, and just before a snap-blackout, we had Iago suddenly look up, confronting the audience with his eyes. Greg wanted the moment to be a strange final aside, enigmatic, open to your own interpretation, but I was always clear about it myself. The dangerous wordsmith may be silent, but in my head this question always rang out:

You saw what was happening – why didn't you stop it?

5 'I nothing, but to please his fantasy' (3.3.303): Amanda Harris as Emilia.

Emilia

AMANDA HARRIS

Amanda Harris won an Olivier award for her performance as Emilia in Gregory Doran's RSC production of *Othello* in 2004; since then she has played Titania in *A Misummer Night's Dream* and Celia in *As You Like It* for the same company. Earlier Shakespearean roles include Desdemona, Emilia in *The Two Noble Kinsmen*, Regan, Buckingham in *Richard III* and Lady Macbeth.

I think I approach tragedy as I approach any other kind of work – according to who I'm playing. The first bearings are always who this person is, what they are after, what their background is, what their story is at the point the play begins. What it is you need to get out of that story determines what method you use, and like most actors I have a range of different techniques that I'll use to get different things out of different characters.

Some of these involve looking at real, historical individuals, and when I was cast by Gregory Doran to play Emilia in *Othello* I started looking, quite early on in the business of reading and thinking and rehearsal, at the case of Ruth Ellis, the last woman ever to be hanged in England. (I don't often tell people what I have used as springboards towards playing a character; in fact I've never mentioned this even to Greg.) Ruth Ellis had nothing to do with the performance I gave as the end-result of the rehearsal process, but it was great to have that sort of post-war, chain-smoking, brandy-drinking, rather loose woman – who was actually quite honourable, by her own lights – as a figure to keep somewhere in mind as Emilia came into focus, in a production whose costumes suggested the early 1950s. I got the RSC to provide me with a videotape of the film made about Ellis in the 1980s, *Dance with a Stranger*, and I read a biography of her, too: the sense of a life prematurely ended, and of relationships lived somewhere on the edge of criminality, and what loucheness was like in the society of that period and where it fitted in, did help. Sometimes the most oblique pieces of apparently unconnected research can be helpful as you find a character; sometimes it is more direct (playing Titania at the moment, for example, I have been rereading lots of fairy tales, and Marina Warner's analyses of them).

But whatever tools I use on the way, what is important from the point of view of the work I need to do as a performer is not the genre but who the character is: in Shakespeare, whether the play has been classed as a comedy, a history or a tragedy, you need to be able to see from one moment to the next that the plot could still turn out differently, and so when I played Regan in *King Lear*, for example, my focus was not on the fact that this woman was going to wind up dead, because she did not know that, but on getting into the mind of a daughter who did not feel loved. She had played at being the brat of the family, after years of being spoiled instead of being loved in the way she wanted to be; she had been given things by her father almost as a way of dismissing her, as we see even in the first scene when he gives her a third of the kingdom but really has his mind on the better share he is planning to give to Cordelia; so I made her consciously naughty, and overtly sexy, and prone to snorting amyl nitrate – which I thought the director would get rid of, but no, she kept it in. As long as it comes from the lines: characters in Shakespeare don't actually exist independently of the things they are given to say and do, however Method-trained performers may sometimes want to pretend otherwise. I remember when I was first in *Othello*, for Cheek by Jowl in 1982, at one early rehearsal the actor playing Othello said, 'I have a problem here – my character just wouldn't say this.' At which the director, Declan Donellan, called a coffee break – quite rightly, as those two had work to do.

Like Regan, with her vicious husband Cornwall and ruthless lover Edmund, Emilia is another Shakespearean character with a very interesting marriage – to Iago, played on this occasion by Antony Sher. Tony and I are great friends, and we had worked together three times before *Othello*, and it was almost surprising how little conscious, deliberate work we had to do on discussing what sort of marriage we were presenting; we slotted into it very readily, partly because we had worked together in the past, and partly because we just seem to work together very easily. We have such fun off stage, nothing like we were on stage in this terrible marriage; we can always giggle and laugh, and know we are safe with each other. We actually did not do that much talking about Iago and Emilia – we did not need to, as each of us could instantly pick up on what the other was doing, and between us we had soon intuited a whole history of the relationship our scenes together were about. Tony is, of course, a fantastic actor (whatever state the honours system may be in, they don't give knighthoods out for nothing in our line of work), and working with someone that good raises your own game, and it feels fantastic. We knew that our Iago and Emilia had loved each other for a bit, flirted with each other quite a lot, probably had great sex, up to a point. But there is something in him which she does not know, and nor does she attempt to analyse whatever it is she may half-guess about it, since there is no point trying to discuss things in this marriage, that isn't how it works. Emilia, in any case, though a bright woman, is not especially articulate. So, in a way, there was no need for Tony and I to discuss this marriage consciously, because we sensed that it was a marriage that was itself based on not discussing things explicitly.

One reason we could get on with our work so productively, finding our sense of this situation flowing as it did, was that our director had done his part of the job so well: Greg Doran came into the show with a strong sense of some of the frameworks and parameters within which this version of the Iago–Emilia marriage was going to work. He always had a very strong sense that his *Othello* needed to place this relationship more centrally than some other productions of the play had done, so that the audience would not see Emilia as Desdemona's confidante first and Iago's wife only incidentally. Both Greg and I were from the first very clear about the fact that we did not want Emilia to be a maidservant, least of all a long-standing lady-in-waiting to Desdemona. Even in being assigned to look after Desdemona she is described first and foremost in terms of her relation to Iago – 'I prithee, let thy wife attend on her', Othello tells him, at 1.3.296 – and there is nothing to suggest that she and Desdemona have even met before. This was very important to me, the sense that the relationship between Desdemona and Emilia only happens during the time depicted in the play and that it is emphatically not, as it sometimes can seem on stage, between a pair of honorary sisters (like that between Helena and Hermia in *A Midsummer Night's Dream*) or between a mistress and an already intimate servant (like that between that other Emilia in *Two Noble Kinsmen*, who I played for the RSC in 1986, and her gentlewoman). Desdemona happens to Emilia: this young, pretty and, from Emilia's perspective, spoiled little thing is thrown upon her, and given the difference between the backgrounds and experiences of life of the pampered newly-wed and the NCO's long-suffering wife, why should we expect Emilia to like her? The first thing Emilia is likely to feel is a lesser dose of just the sort of destructive envy that is her husband's speciality: this young heiress is having a good time, and she is not. What is so marvellous about the role of Emilia, though, slight and incidental as it can look, is the way in which you can see her coming to care for Desdemona, developing an almost maternal, honourable warmth towards her over the play's action, until she finds herself dying to vindicate her.

So in the first scene in which we see both of them on stage at once – and not exactly together, in our production – we hinted at a certain initial antagonism on Emilia's part. In 2.1, when they arrive in Cyprus after the storm, we had Desdemona stage right, with Cassio and Montano fussing around her and getting her coffee from a flask and Iago flirting with her and improvising his little misogynist poem (at 2.1.132–63), while I stayed mainly stage left, putting in those interesting, bitter little replies to Iago's implied slanders about my domestic behaviour but being substantially ignored. At our entrance together, 2.1.84–6, where Montano tells his assembled staff to pretty much worship Desdemona ('You men of Cyprus, let her have your knees', 85), Emilia had been gratified by the way that it was actually her eye that all the soldiers caught rather than Desdemona's, because they could see that she was the sassy one, the good-time girl, but after that she had been cut out of the conversation among her social superiors and at best ignored by her husband. So there she is, watching Iago being all sweet and amusing with Desdemona (when she has heard all these anti-feminist jokes of his a thousand times before, and has had to live with them), after a voyage during which she has been seasick yet again on the way to yet another distant posting to yet another dreary block of married quarters, while Desdemona has been all girlish excitement at the prospect of seeing her new husband again. So, of course, Emilia is feeling pretty sour, and what we evolved as a piece of business to express this was have Emilia try to deflect Iago's flirtation with Desdemona by coming almost rudely across the stage and pouring a tot of brandy into Desdemona's coffee, just as Iago's poem is building towards a climax. It's a gesture which looks ostensibly helpful or companionable towards Desdemona, but which really makes just the same hostile, levelling comment which the audience will hear later in this scene from Iago – 'The wine she drinks is made of grapes' (2.1.251–2). When Othello then arrives and she sees him pouring out all that love-poetry over Desdemona, she may at one level be quite excited by it, as though these people are living in one of the romantic novels she reads, but mainly she just thinks these are two people who have it undeservedly easy, being embarrassingly smug in public.

In the following scene, 2.3, thanks to Greg rather than to Shakespeare, we got to see Emilia much more in her own element. Greg had decided even before rehearsals started that despite her sorry omission from the script at this point he wanted Emilia to be present at the party among the sentries, where Iago gets Cassio drunk: in fact when he telephoned me to ask if I wanted to play the role, he told me he wanted to do this, as if to supply an added incentive. Of course, he didn't need to – I was very keen to work with Tony again anyway, and with Greg – but the idea immediately made sense to me, so much so that I started to jump perilously up and down in the bath with excitement. I already knew the play very well, having played Desdemona in 1982, and it immediately seemed to me that putting Emilia into that scene could really go a long way towards telling her story, showing who she was, establishing her real milieu. She is the wife of a non-commissioned officer, someone used above all to being around uniformed men, and, as we could show by having her around as a kind of mistress of ceremonies at that drunken gathering, about the only pleasure in her life is that of flirting with soldiers. Just flirting, mind; Iago's paranoid fantasies about her being unfaithful with his colleagues were clearly just that; but they did come out of the circumstances of the life this military couple actually lived, which that drinking scene really enabled us to illustrate in a way which I think made the production's depiction of their marriage much more comprehensible and much richer than it often is. The really sad thing we showed in that scene was a woman who has got slightly drunk and thinks she is having a good time with her husband, to the extent of joining in the men's game of pulling down Cassio's trousers when they have deliberately got him plastered, but when she then crosses to Iago and hopes to get amorous he doesn't want to know, because, as the audience have seen, he thinks she has gone too far, thinks that this debagging of Cassio just confirms his worst suspicions. In any case, he has to get on with incriminating Cassio instead of giving her any attention, and he dismisses her with real anger. It was my idea, the debagging (I did play Stiffie Byng in *Jeeves*, after all), and I am very proud of it. It came very naturally, in rehearsal – it was one of those places where Tony and I would come off stage and laugh together with a kind of delight at having got it so right. It so fleshed out their shared story that it almost seemed to give the audience as much insight into their life together as all their other scenes put together.

That sense of their shared marital past at all those other barracks over the years gave a really useful preparation for Emilia's little soliloquy in 3.3, when she picks up the handkerchief Desdemona has dropped and says she is going to comply with her husband's request to give it to him (294–303). In lots of productions of *Othello* I think that speech can look very odd and contrived – as though the plot needs Emilia to supply Iago with the handkerchief, but that she has so far looked like such an obedient servant and well-meaning friend to Desdemona that you would not think she could really bring herself to do so. With us, I think, it was clear that Iago and Emilia had habitually colluded in various petty crimes against his military superiors during their marriage – fiddling the till in the NAAFI, that sort of thing – and furthermore that there was an odd way in which their own love-life together was blocked (hence all her flirting with other men, and smoking, and drinking) and she was resigned almost to pimping for him to maintain her hold and to keep his interest. It's a grey area, and the text does not give you too explicit a lead, but there does seem to be an undertone in that speech of Emilia thinking, 'Well, he clearly fancies Desdemona, I'll humour it, I might get something out of it myself.' It is very much a working relationship, theirs; each knows the other's habitual strategies, they are used to deliberately ignoring certain things about each other, but they have always worked together for their mutual advantage, even in quite grubby ways. In rehearsal Tony and I nicknamed them Mr and Mrs Filch. I had a vague notion that she had been running a pub when she met him, he perhaps one of her customers, but had been willing to give it up and marry him partly because the pub was failing due to her drinking the profits and giving too many free drinks. Once you have established the fact, in any event, that her main loyalty is to her marriage, and that the life she has always known revolves around Iago's barracks rather than Desdemona's boudoir, then, of course, her material interest is going to be in backing up Iago's latest underhand rule-bending scheme, whatever it may be, rather than in looking after Desdemona's haberdashery.

So Emilia's ultimate decision to shop Iago to the authorities in 5.2 carried all the more weight: that's the one thing which, up until now, neither would ever have done to the other, but she has now experienced this appalling revelation that Iago has completely exceeded the code of honour among thieves by which their marriage has so far survived. That shared semi-criminal bond also helped explain, I think, why Emilia had not realized earlier what Iago had been doing. Again, in some performances of *Othello* I have seen, Emilia can seem unbelievably naïve and stupid – she guesses that somebody has been maligning Desdemona ('I will be hanged if some eternal villain . . . have not devised this slander', she says, 4.2.134–7), she is married to somebody transparently wicked and devious, but she fails to put two and two together. Whereas in our version it is precisely because Emilia knows that, up to a point, her Iago is a criminal that she does not suspect him: she knows about the embezzlement and the theft and whatever else, she has been in on it, but she thinks she knows that he would never go significantly further. We showed the audience one aspect of how thoroughly Emilia and Iago did understand each other, then, so that we could equally show how much she had never guessed about him, and one thing Tony and I did talk purposefully and explicitly about was the extent of her innocence of his psychosis. I remember one day in rehearsal when Tony actually asked me to stop watching his soliloquies, in case my knowledge of what he was doing in them should colour my performance as Emilia, and he was quite right: it is vital that she should guess nothing of that side of him, until the complete, traumatic horror of the last scene. So there are real limits to her knowledge of him: hence when she first sees him wearing lieutenant's stripes after being promoted in Cassio's place, in fact when she finds his old ensign's stripes left on stage at the start of the second half in 3.4, she clearly thinks to herself, 'Oh, I wonder what that's all about?', but she doesn't ask questions: she is more used to staying out of his way in affairs like that, and anaesthetizing herself by reading bad romantic novels. She is used above all to waiting about – reading magazines about movie stars, eating chocolates, stubbing out cigarettes in empty tubs of Pond's cold cream.

What she is instead doing over the course of the intervening scenes is finding an increasing, protective warmth towards Desdemona, and that was again very easy to work on in rehearsal because I did indeed, as myself, become very friendly with our Desdemona, Lisa Dillon – just as it was also very easy to resent her in the early scenes of the play, she being so sickeningly young and gorgeous and posh and a prize-winning good girl straight out of RADA and all! However Emilia resents having the job foisted on her of doing some of this heiress's domestic work for her at the beginning of the play, she comes to see Desdemona as a fellow-sufferer, someone who has just embarked on what starts to look like potentially just as abusive a marriage as her own. There was one day, I remember, sitting in the green room, when Tony and I were eating one of those sad microwaved meals that actors get so used to, and he suddenly asked, 'Have I beaten you?' and I immediately said, 'Yes.' It took no discussion; that was just how we both knew how things were between our Mr and Mrs Filch; he didn't beat her constantly, or even as though he was that inter-ested in it, but every now and then he got very angry, and furiously jealous. And now this hard-bitten woman, her marriage a matter of survival strategies and cigarette ends, has this lovely young girl put into her charge – and however cynical and aloof she feels at first, she finds herself identifying with her. And even if Emilia can see no way out of her unsatisfactory life for herself, she does not want Desdemona to go down the same road that she has travelled or find herself living in the same kind of marital trap. That is the side of Emilia that makes her so lovable, that warmth of character, that gen-erosity of spirit which makes her so completely unlike her husband, whose passionate interest in other people is entirely destructive. That is why they should clearly never have got married: she is a good-time girl who has been willing to dibble and dabble in the shady side of things, but her strongest instincts are benevolent, so that she will take someone like Desdemona under her wing once she gets to know and understand her and realizes she is all right. It is very interesting, I think, that she and Iago have no children – obviously, that is partly because that wasn't the kind of story Shakespeare was concentrat-ing on telling in *Othello*, and except in the matter of Desdemona's divided loyalties to her father and her new husband this just is not a play about parenthood, but as an actor you have to pursue it and motivate it and make sense of it in terms of the character any-way. Emilia, childless and unhappily married, practically adopts Desdemona as a daughter, transfers onto her that fully, which helps explain her crucial, and, as it turns out, self-destructive, intervention in the final scene of the play.

That only gets really articulated, though, almost at the last minute, in the willow-song scene, 4.3. That was a scene I always intensely enjoyed playing, partly because it was such a delight to work with Lisa, but partly because it is such a busy, active scene to play. It is a wonderful piece of writing in the way in which the bond between the two women, as well as being hinted at in their conversation, is shown in and through the sheer practicality of this shared part of their lives: the taking off of the socks, the helping her off with her earrings. 'Shall I go fetch your nightgown?' 'No. Unpin me here' (33). The very ordinariness and matter-of-factness of this intimacy makes it so very real and makes its imminent destruction so much more tragic: and the other superb thing about the dialogue in this scene is that although there is such a strong sense of something awful in the air, of both women knowing in their hearts how awful the situation is, neither can quite say so explicitly. Just as Emilia has never fully admitted to herself how bad her marriage has been – she would have left if she had – so she is not, at this point anyway, going to say openly how appalled she is beginning to be by what is happening between Desdemona and Othello. 'I would you had never seen him' (17), she blurts, but gives no further explanation, especially when Desdemona then defends him and changes the subject. What we played in this scene was how surprised these women are to confide in each other as much as they do: Desdemona really had dismissed Emilia at line 56, 'Go, get thee gone. Good night', but she had lingered in the doorway, hearing Desdemona sighing and almost in tears, and it was in response to Emilia's return, to comfort her, that Desdemona came out with 'Mine eyes do itch. Doth that bode weeping?' It was only then that Desdemona, turning to this older, worldlier woman, asked her a question far more intimate than anything that had passed between them before – about whether infidelity ever really happened – and Emilia at last has what is clearly a heartfelt outburst, about how if husbands mistreat their wives they should expect to be mistreated in return. This evens the score between them, somehow, each has had a go at comforting the other, and now Emilia really can go – leaving Desdemona, as instructed, at her husband's mercy.

After that very painful, but delicate, scene, as Emilia you still have the last scene to come, in which you have to play as intense a trauma as anything in drama – the realization that your husband, whom you still at some level love, who almost to the last you think will be able to explain everything away and establish his innocence ('I know thou didst not. Thou'rt not such a villain. / Speak, for my heart is full', 5.2.181–2), is a psychotic, a murderer, and you have even helped him commit these atrocious crimes. The one person she thought she could still protect from the sorts of nastiness her life has been full of, Desdemona, has been killed – she failed her – and killed, moreover, by that stupid Othello. Emilia may at one point have found Othello quite attractive (though less so than Lodovico, incidentally – I always thought that Emilia's 'I know a lady of Venice would have walked barefoot to Palestine for a touch of his nether lip', 4.3.36–7, was a disguised confession), but by now she had already come to think of him as just another, lesser version of her own husband – someone who ignores her, and is infinitely better with the troops than with women, and does not even have Iago's useful pragmatism. Now whatever she may have excused in Othello has gone, and he is just a dupe, more stupid in preferring anything to Desdemona's life than she could ever have imagined, a murderous coxcomb, as ignorant as dirt; the dupe, moreover, of Iago, who suddenly she realizes is so much worse even than that. It is a realization which, being the woman she is, she experiences not just as an idea but physically: 'Villainy, villainy, villainy! / I think upon't, I think. I smell't. O villainy!' (5.2.197–8).

This knowledge is so horrible that she cannot imagine being able to live with it: 'I'll kill myself for grief', are her next words, but after she manages fifty lines later to give her crucial evidence about how Iago obtained the handkerchief, Iago saves her the trouble – and in our production, that act of violence was made the more shocking by being also sexual. The audience had already seen Iago failing to finish off Cassio in the previous scene because he was obsessively trying to castrate him first (hence his wound being in the leg, which is otherwise surprising), and now his loathing, as if of sexuality itself, drove him to stab Emilia, as Montano held back Othello from trying to kill him, not in the heart but upward between the legs. This was a horrible moment, as it should be, but actually led to one of the funniest incidents between Tony and me in rehearsal. When we were first attempting that sequence of moves, leading to him making that upward stab (though at that stage with no knife), we almost got quite balletic, trying different slight variants of relative positioning and of angle, and when he had got it as I thought right, we repeated it, over and over again, with me crying out, 'Yes, that's it! That's it!' I suddenly realized that all the stage managers were falling about laughing, because of course we looked like some terrible pornographic movie. We actually had to take a whole day off from that scene after that, because we would be laughing too much to do it every time the murder came around. It got less balletic as we worked with it, uglier, the concentrated hatred it made visible ever more frightening. It was surprisingly easy to act what remained, I found, without needing to analyse too much what was going through Emilia's mind as she bled to death; her instinct was to join her beloved Desdemona, to get close to her body, as if to recapitulate that little moment of mutual comfort in the willow-song scene. Sometimes you just know what to do, without needing to think about it. Very young performers can often play material which deals with experiences they are too young to have had because their imaginations somehow know about it already, and it can be like that playing a death: you have never died yourself, but somehow you know this is how it would be.

What makes Emilia's death so powerful for the audience – or so I hope – is the way in which it looks so contingent, so like something that did not need to happen to her: Othello, by contrast, always did see himself as a character in a great operatic story, he just did not recognize early enough that it was a tragedy, whereas Emilia is at heart a good woman and ought by rights to have been a comic survivor. I imagine that that's one reason Greg cast me in this part, because I love playing comedy, and always have an instinct towards it. In fact the trajectory of rehearsals was that I started off by playing her much more broadly, more twinkly, almost camp, as a way into the warmth of this person, before toning that down into what I hope was something convincingly real, finding the other side, the darker side. All Shakespeare's tragedies stay open to comedy, they have to, and vice versa. Rehearsing me as Titania in *A Midsummer Night's Dream* the following season, Greg said that to bring out the sparkling diamond of the comedy, it had to be set against a black background – that if we are to enjoy the love and happiness in the play, the pain and the threat have to be absolutely genuine – and, of course, the contrary applies to *Othello*: for the darkness of the tragedy to be made visible, the sparkling possibility of happiness has to be there to set it off. Emilia is part of that sparkle, and her extinction is for me a very big part of that tragedy.

6   Perplexed in the extreme: Nonso Anozie as Othello.

Othello

NONSO ANOZIE

Nonso Anozie played the title role in Cheek by Jowl's production of *Othello* in 2004, for which he won that year's Ian Charleson Award; on the production's international tour he was also the first non-Chinese actor to win the Magnolia Award in China. He had received a special commendation in the 2003 Ian Charleson awards for his performance in the title role in Declan Donellan's RSC Academy production of *King Lear*. His other theatre experience includes *Edmond* at the National, *World Music* at the Crucible in Sheffield, and *Sundance* at the Royal Albert Hall. He made his feature-film debut in *The Last Legion* (2006), with Colin Firth and Ben Kingsley.

The year 2004 was, quite simply, a life-changing one for me. At the age of twenty-five, in the space of eleven months, I travelled the collective distance equivalent of three and a half times around the earth, and gave almost two hundred performances as Othello across five continents and in twenty-two cities. Talk about 'an extravagant and wheeling stranger / Of here and everywhere'! No one ever tells you how difficult and challenging something like this is going to be because very few people really ever do it: they may speculate or give you their best educated guess, but nothing can prepare you either for the experience of inhabiting a role this titanic or that of taking it right across the world.

When I first found out that I had been given the opportunity to play the Moor of Venice, I was filled with many thoughts and emotions: excitement and anticipation that I would have the opportunity to carve my own mark on a truly great character alongside a select few actors that have come before me, but also a feeling of apprehension. Being a relatively young actor (in comparison to most previous Othellos), I was undoubtedly going to be put under close scrutiny in performance, since as with all the great Shakespearean tragic roles Othello comes with its baggage on how it should and should not be done. However, the one thing in which I was resolute was that I would face the challenge of playing Shakespeare's black general head on.

I did at least come to the part with previous experience of playing in Shakespearean tragedy, and in older roles at that. My first-ever job on leaving drama school, in 2002, had been the title role in *King Lear*, in a production directed for the new RSC Academy (an all-newcomer company within the RSC) by the award-winning director and founder of Cheek by Jowl, Declan Donellan. In the middle of the fifth week of rehearsal for *King Lear* I realized that Declan had stopped giving me any rehearsal notes. As a young actor on my first job this gave me cause for concern. Had the director taken a dislike to me? Did he suddenly realize he had made a mistake in casting me in the lead, or was he about to ditch the whole production? Just as I had decided to talk to him about it, he pulled me aside and gave me the news that the reason he had not given me any notes was that he was juggling with the idea of me playing Othello for his own company Cheek by Jowl, and that offering me that role would be the best way of letting me know what he thought of the work I was doing as Lear. So not long after getting used to the idea of playing Shakespeare's aging monarch I was faced with the additional prospect of taking on his Moor!

For much of that year I put the idea of playing Othello to the back of my mind, as I had the task of Lear at hand. But slowly but surely word spread that I was going to be Cheek by Jowl's Othello, and whenever I met an actor or director who had worked on the play or even just seen it they would throw in their ten-pence-worth as to what I should think about doing when I played the role. I also started to realize what a huge history this part carried, what an accumulation of past productions and critical essays there was, and what strong feelings the play evoked around the question of how it deals with race. I met another black actor, who shall remain nameless, who went so far as to tell me that 'a black man cannot play Othello'. But I wasn't about to refuse this challenge, and instead I simply decided from then onwards to block out anything and everything to do with other people's opinions about Othello. If I were going to do a job of playing the Moor that I could be proud of, I would have to please only myself and my own artistic integrity. This way it would at least be my Othello, and I wouldn't be distracted from engaging fully with the part by any suspicion that I either was or should be rehashing someone else's ideas about what he should be. I decided to approach the play as though it had never been done before, as if it were a new, undiscovered work of Shakespeare. This was made easier for me than it might have been for an older actor in that I had only ever seen one theatre production of *Othello*, the 1999 RSC production, with Ray Fearon in the title role.

The only real preparation I decided to do for the role was to learn the entire part before rehearsals began, a procedure which Declan urged on the whole company. This way I would not have the added hindrance of a script in my hand once rehearsals began. I was very careful to learn the script in a cold and clinical fashion, so as not to develop patterns in speech that would be hard to break later on. Othello speaks almost entirely in verse, so I kept this simplicity of learning the lines by sticking rigidly to the iambic pentameter. This helped me by preventing any of my own speech patterns from emerging before rehearsals, and also, unexpectedly, this process stapled the heartbeat of the play (the iamb) into my mind, so that no matter how much I appeared (later on in rehearsals) to stray from the *ti tum ti tum* of the iambic pentameter, it would always be there, much like a jazz singer improvising over the unchanging beat of the music. The singer may seem to go off on a tangent, but because of a complete understanding of the role of the music and indeed her own the singer will (if she so chooses) start, pause and finish with the music. This, I believe, should be the actor's relationship to Shakespeare's magical verse.

When rehearsals started in January of 2004 I felt – for lack of a better word – quite naked. This was because I didn't have any preconceptions about the play. I was totally open to my Othello becoming anything that rehearsals might throw up. At the time it felt strange that the very thing that gave me confidence in my approach to the play should now evoke such feelings of awkwardness. But this soon changed as I found out that everyone else in the cast was in the same boat, and indeed the first thing that Declan said when addressing the whole company was that, even though he had directed it just over twenty years earlier, he did not know how he was going to tackle this, the most 'poetic' of Shakespeare's tragedies. I very quickly took comfort in the fact that this experience was going to be a voyage of discovery for the entire company and not just me.

The first week of rehearsal was used to warm us up to working with each other. This was done by playing familiar and not-so-familiar improvisation and concentration (attention) games. At first there was a lack of interest in these games, as everyone involved was very keen to get to grips with the text since we had a very short rehearsal period, only six weeks. This soon subsided, however, as we all started to become more comfortable with each other, and indeed these company-forming exercises put us into a much better place to start work on the play.

Declan's instruction that we should all be 'off book' before we began was very useful, since, as I have seen in my theatre experience, actors are only human and have many insecurities like anyone else (if not more!), and will often find themselves using the book in their hand as a shield for this. With your eyes buried in the script on a rehearsal-room floor, it is easier to avoid eye contact and also physical contact with the other actors. As any psychologist will tell you, when a person is nervous a common reaction is to avoid eye contact. This would seem like a very obvious thing to say, and many actors would say that it is in their 'process' to have a book in their hand during early rehearsals, so that they can take in the script and a sense of the movements and the other players at the same time. However, in my own experience that practice does not start the rehearsal process from a good place. The essence of drama comes in the contact between the actors, and it is somewhere in that genuine intimacy that lies the very elusive thing that nobody can put their finger on but everyone wants to see when they go to the theatre. If you stop this thing from developing from the very start of the creative process, then the chances are that you will always be missing something from the production, always held back by a mental sense that you are somewhere on a remembered page rather than in the action.

The first thing any drama student learns is that drama is conflict between two or more entities. This conflict or tension can be external, experienced between people on stage, or internal, experienced as conflicting thoughts within an individual. During our rehearsal period it was this conflict that was sought out in every facet of the play. After spending most of the day working on the verse we would be directed to read or 'do' the play with no guidelines as to what was expected of us. After 'doing' the play or scene Declan would go through what he liked or didn't like and we would then do it again. This goes on three or four more times, and then Declan starts to look for the conflict in the play by inviting us to 'raise the stakes'. More than anyone else I have worked with, Declan is most concerned with what is going on between the actors on stage. He is not overly concerned with the set or musical accompaniment. He would get us to raise the stakes in the scene by advising us to really see what our characters had to win or lose in every scene and indeed on every line. In doing this, just as defining your objective tells you what your character is trying to do to a person or persons in a scene, seeing what is at stake for your character to win or lose in the scene literally changes what you say and do on stage every time you play that passage. This in turn raises the stakes still further, and can be incredible to watch. This is something Declan learned originally from reading Stanislavsky and experimenting with his ideas in rehearsal, and he describes it in his book *The Actor and the Target* (2004): it can sound almost formulaic, but it is much easier said than done and is something that comes to you rather than something that can be harnessed by deliberate willpower alone.

As rehearsals went on I started to develop my ideas of the story of *Othello* as a play, the character of Othello and his relationships with the other characters on stage, especially those with Desdemona and Iago. *Othello* at first may seem quite complicated, but when broken down it is a very simple story indeed. A and B are in love. C observes this relationship and for reasons that are never fully revealed sets up a series of situations that eventually lead not only to the breakdown of this relationship but to the death of both A and B. Of course A and B are Othello and Desdemona and Iago is the envious C. This was the simplest way in which I could break down the story. Once you break down the story in such a way it gives you the flexibility to do whatever comes to you, as long as you stick to the principal story.

The character of Othello is certainly one of the richest in Shakespeare's writing. I got to grips with it by firstly taking note of what was said to him, and about him, and also what he himself says, highlighting a selection of what seemed to me to be key phrases:
- 'the sooty bosom / Of such a thing as thou' (Brabantio to Othello, 1.2.70–1)
- 'little of this great world can I speak / More than pertains to feats of broil and battle' (Othello, 1.3.86–7)
- 'To fall in love with what she feared to look on' (Brabantio, 1.3.98)
- 'Your son-in-law is far more fair than black' (Duke of Venice, 1.3.290)

- 'It gives me wonder great as my content / To see you here before me. O my soul's joy' (Othello to Desdemona, 2.1.185)
- 'Our noble and valiant General' (Herald, 2.2.1)
- ''Zounds, if I once stir . . . the best of you shall sink in my rebuke' (Othello, 2.3.200–2)
- 'Her name . . . is now begrimed and black as mine own face' (Othello, 3.3.391–3)
- 'the nature / Whom passion could not shake, whose solid virtue / The shot of accident nor dart of chance / Could neither graze nor pierce' (Lodovico about Othello, 4.1.266–9)
- 'Should I repent me . . . where is that Promethean heat . . . this sorrow's heavenly . . . have you prayed tonight?' (Othello, 5.2.10, 12, 21, 26)
- 'I took by th' throat the circumcisèd dog' (Othello, 5.2.364)

Even from these short quotations we can start to build a picture of Othello's character. We can see that he is a black man of very dark skin, and that being black in the society and time of the play's setting was likely to be regarded far more negatively than is being black and part of a minority today. We can see that he is considered by both the state and himself to be valiant and noble, and the evidence also reveals that he must be an incredibly skilled soldier in both armed and unarmed combat. He is a man who is highly regarded as someone with an unshakable resolve, someone who possesses the ability to control his temper under enormous pressure. Othello is someone who is truthfully and honestly in love and is very well equipped to express his love verbally and indeed physically. He is also extremely well educated and well travelled, and, probably as a result of his travels, he has encountered many religions. I reached the conclusion that although he is (at present) a Christian of some sort, he must have converted from some other faith, perhaps Judaism or more likely Islam – there's a special bitterness in the way in which he identifies with that 'circumcisèd dog' as he kills himself. As we can see, Othello is an incredibly rich character.

Now, as I look back at how I built Othello, I can speak more objectively about something that was taking place naturally and almost unconsciously (in the early stages of rehearsal) but was central to the character I was building. Down the long stage history of *Othello*, many more white actors than black have played the title character. Some of the most famous of these performances, such as Olivier's, were noted for the actor's ability to capture Othello's 'otherness', their ability to lower their voices, change their physicality and blacken their skin to simulate what they perceived as being black or 'other'. I am black, so I have, for free, all of those things that white actors had to spend time working on before getting to grips with the story of the play and Othello's relationships with the other characters, and I suspect that this made me a less apparently narcissistic or self-regarding Othello than the anxiously make-up-covered creature offered by some of my white predecessors. I did do a large amount of physical and vocal work to present a general with the life history that Othello has, but not nearly as much as I would have had to do had I had to change my race. This allowed me to concentrate on the most important aspect of Othello. Although Othello is black, strong, intelligent, valiant and noble, in my eyes the most important thing about him is that he is a man in love and that from the moment the play starts he feels he would be nothing without his relationship to Desdemona. This is quite evident from the outset: among the first things we hear him say are 'I love the gentle Desdemona' (1.2.25), and that he would never have relinquished his bachelorhood for anyone else. This fact was at the centre of my Othello, and I believe is what contributed to him becoming far more believable than if I had largely concentrated on his status as a racial outsider. This also starts the character in a very good place for the actor to chart Othello's emotional decline thereafter; it also makes his final action of killing his wife and then himself infinitely more plausible.

It goes without saying that the relationship between Othello and Iago is strange, to say the least. How is it possible that this low-ranking officer even has such intimate dialogues with a general, let alone the heated exchanges depicted in the play, which could easily result in Iago's demotion, beating or even execution? I liken their relationship to that of a crocodile and the tiniest scavenger bird. In the wild the crocodile is a ferocious and feared predator and would make a light snack of the scavenger bird, but chooses not to. The scavenger bird picks waste food from in between the teeth of an appreciative crocodile. The bird is well fed, and the crocodile has clean teeth. Because of this mutual benefit, they have the most unusual of relationships. In the same way, Othello must have benefited from Iago's apparent honesty and cunning intelligence in the past, and Iago has, of course, gained some perks (though obviously not enough) from being highly favoured by the general. This relationship and its benign counterpart, the loving marriage with Desdemona, are arguably the most important in the play: the whole plot depends on both being completely believable, since otherwise no audience will accept the gory body count at the play's conclusion. Maintaining these relationships was at the heart of being able to keep this play fresh, and I found them very enjoyable to play.

The thing that people always told me they had found hard to take in past productions of Othello was that they could not believe that Othello could be intelligent enough to speak such well-constructed verse and yet also be foolish enough to fall into Iago's trap. I would contend, however, that it is precisely Othello's intelligence, coupled with his other honourable qualities, that make him who he is and make him susceptible to falling blindly into Iago's web. Othello has had to overcome impossible odds to achieve and uphold the position of general in the Venetian army; he has probably had to work many times harder than his white counterparts, with many people opposing his progression upwards through the ranks. As a result of this unusual life choice, I feel that Othello has had to develop an impervious imaginary armour. This armour (intelligence, guile, honesty, strength and willpower, all directed towards maintaining his professional superiority and cool) has served him well until now, protecting his unseen, more vulnerable side from predators, and in the sphere of his military career it has kept Iago's talons at bay. Unfortunately, from the outset of the play we can see that Othello is in love with Desdemona and has brought her close to his vulnerable side, by-passing his shield (probably for the first time), creating a chink in his armour. Iago in his cunning easily spots this weakness, and attacks Othello from its source, Desdemona. In striking Othello's love he not only unsettles the giant general (which could arguably be his sole aim, initially) but, as it transpires, destroys him.

Othello has been the biggest challenge I have had in my acting career so far and he grew very personal to me as rehearsals went on. I suppose this was due to the amount of time I spent discovering and building him. Anything that is precious and that you have had to work for will obviously make you feel attached to it. This manifested itself during the touring of the play, in a kind of Othello-like possessiveness, but in the end it only served to teach me that you cannot own a character. You simply have your time with them and move on.

As the rehearsal period drew to a close, I was remarkably relaxed about opening the show to a foreign audience. Something about us performing in an unknown country prevented me from picturing us performing, resulting in this relaxed frame of mind. I suppose as actors we would all want to be calm before a show, but for me to be as laid-back as I was is very unusual. This soon changed, as on the night before we opened (at the Théâtre du Nord in Lille, France), I had what could only be described as a rude awakening. For one night, I experienced what it might be like to be an insomniac. I was kept awake that night by the alarm bells in my head that clearly rang out 'First night!!!' It had suddenly dawned on me that if we opened the play the following night and the audience and press alike hated the show and 'my' Othello, then we could potentially spend the next year of our lives performing in a production that we did not believe in. I spent the majority of that night in prayer. The next day I came to the quick realization that the play was not under my control and that I would have to let the work that we as a company had done speak for itself. I also had to relinquish ownership of the character, so that I could walk away from praise or criticism without taking it too personally. Regardless of my previous fears, the show went very well on opening night and was subsequently well received nationwide and, indeed, worldwide.

That performance space where we first opened was very large. The auditorium seated just over one thousand people and the stage itself was about six times the size of the room that we had been rehearsing in just three days earlier. Our next performance space (the Théâtre National in Paris) also seated around a thousand people, and felt huge. After that we were performing in a space almost as small as our rehearsal room. Later on in the tour we would travel from places where the temperature in the shade was 45 degrees centigrade to places where the temperature was below freezing. This aspect of the tour was something that you cannot really prepare for, as adapting to different performance spaces and climate change is something you can only do as it happens. This proved to be very tough when we flew on a twenty-four-hour flight from Australia to London, with barely a week's rest before flying to Poland to start a three-week tour of

Eastern Europe. You just don't know how that will affect you until you do it.

Othello was, and still is, a character that slowly reveals more about himself the longer I spend with him. Even as I have been writing this piece I see more things that I could have explored in performance. This was something that I exploited during the year-long run of this play. I took as many opportunities as I could to bring out new aspects of the Moor as they unfolded to me. I think Othello is one of those few roles that I feel I would be able to return to in later life and play differently every time. I will always, weirdly, be able to look both back and forward to my relationship with the elusive black general, Othello.

Macbeth

7 'Yet here's a spot . . .' (5.1.30): Sian Thomas as Lady Macbeth.

Lady Macbeth

SIAN THOMAS

Sian Thomas played Lady Macbeth in Dominic Cooke's 2004 RSC production of *Macbeth*, at the same time as playing Gertrude in Michael Boyd's *Hamlet*: previous RSC roles include Goneril and Katharina, and she has also played Desdemona. She has worked extensively at the Glasgow Citizens, at the National, at the Young Vic and at the Lyric Hammersmith, and won an award for Best Actress for her performance in the Renaissance Theatre Company production of *Uncle Vanya*. In other media, she has appeared in *Inspector Morse*, on *Book of the Week*, and in *Prick Up Your Ears*.

Of all the roles I have played outside the Shakespeare canon, very few draw on the same registers as Lady Macbeth. Hedda Gabler has similarities, and I was reminded of her a few times while playing Lady Macbeth. But I cannot think of much that has been written since Ibsen that has that same resonance. I am very lucky to live with Tony Harrison, who is a fine critic as well as a major poet and translator (not least of Greek tragedy). When I first got cast in this role I raided his shelves, and read wonderful essays on *Macbeth* by Coleridge, and Hazlitt, and looked at whatever else I could find: A. C. Bradley, who is still very useful (partly because he thinks psychologically about character, as an actor needs to), and Wilson Knight, right up to Wilbur Sanders and M. M. Mahood, and Frank Kermode and Harold Bloom. And of course with much of it I would think, 'Oh, rubbish!', or, 'I'm not persuaded by this', or, 'I can't use this', but I just wanted to spread my nets and find out as much as I could. Then, once you have done that as an actor, you need to start forgetting it all, so that you still come to the part freshly, as if neither you nor anyone else has played it before.

Except, in this instance, one great actress from the past. Coleridge and Hazlitt stayed with me as I studied the part, and this was very appropriate, because I found myself influenced by accounts of a performer they both watched and admired, Sarah Siddons. It was not planned, and in some ways the rest of the costume design of our production – which looked quite Russian, and if anything early twentieth-century – did not have this in mind at all, but I wound up looking quite consciously like the famous Henry Fuseli painting of Siddons as Lady Macbeth in the sleepwalking scene. I was thrilled about this when I realized, because I am a great fan of hers: I have a long-standing interest in her work, and indeed have a number of contemporary prints of her all over my house. There is a wonderful description of her Lady Macbeth, by Hazlitt, which I read quite late on in the rehearsal process, when it was time to settle various decisions, and I found it very extraordinary to find how many of the choices we had made were the same as she had in her own interpretation two centuries earlier. She had wanted to play Lady Macbeth not as an evil queen but as a vulnerable, real woman, even down to wanting her to be fragile and blonde. She was not either of those things herself – she was a rather Junoesque brunette – and was quite upset not to be able to look as frail as she thought Lady Macbeth should be. Siddons thought Lady Macbeth needed to call on the spirits to unsex her (at 1.5.39–53) because she was not naturally ruthless or masculine at all, and that was very much how I had come to see her, too.

Many smaller details about how Siddons played particular moments tallied with the way in which I saw Lady Macbeth. During her first speech, when Lady Macbeth is reading her husband's letter about the witches, Siddons had apparently made a special point of sounding imaginatively touched by his account of their powers: on 'They made themselves air' (1.5.4–5) she gave quite a pause before the word 'air' – 'They made themselves (*looks up, pause, slightly breathy*) – air.' Yes, I thought, I'll try that, too. And I took the same solution as Siddons to one famous question of emphasis posed in 1.7, when in response to Macbeth's question, 'If we should fail?' she replies, 'We fail' (1.7.59– 60). There are so many ways of saying those two monosyllables, with such different worlds of implication: it can be a question, either suddenly apprehensive about the possibility of failure or completely dismissing the very idea ('We . . fail?', or 'We fail?!', or '*We*, fail??'), or it can be a quick fatalistic shrug, or all sorts of shades in between. Siddons played it quite matter-of-fact, but with an underlying excitement, so that the two words made a plain undaunted statement – if we fail, we fail, but so what? Let's do it anyway. This fitted perfectly with my sense of Lady Macbeth – as someone who saw the murder of Duncan as her one clear chance to escape from being the timid, domestic creature she was afraid she might be – and that is how I played 'We fail', too.

Siddons was also the first performer, so far as we know, to put down the candle she carried on for the sleepwalking scene. Everyone does this now (it's hard to do much in the way of miming washing your hands if you are clutching a naked flame!), but at the time it was a revelation, and freed her up tremendously to make that scene one of the most exciting she ever played. I felt a great sense of Siddons being with me on the press night of our production. I gave an interview that day, at the RSC's little gallery and museum beside the Swan Theatre in Stratford, and noticed that I was standing in front of a glass case containing the slippers which Siddons had worn in the sleepwalking scene the last time she ever played it. I rather liked the idea that I was playing this role for her, as a sort of continuation of what she did – as if I was here being the small-boned, fragile, feminine, blonde Lady Macbeth she always wanted to be.

I think it is impossible to play Lady Macbeth as just an evil bitch, the 'fiend-like queen' referred to in the propaganda of the regime which supplants hers. From the start I knew I would be playing her as vulnerable, and once you grasp that as a starting point, you find she is also incredibly brave: considering she is not naturally as hard as nails, her willpower is extraordinary. In one of the essays I read, Wilbur Sanders talks about something Nietzsche defined called 'strong pessimism' (it's in *The Dramatist and the Received Idea*, 1968), and I found this very fascinating and suggestive. He describes it as a kind of moral vertigo, where you are beyond moral judgement, way beyond the concepts of good and bad: a potent dynamism and life force that lies underneath what we perceive as evil. It is a need to live, to make something happen, even if that means going beyond the frontiers of morality, and this poor woman Lady Macbeth has no means of making anything happen; when we first meet her she is utterly frustrated, for she has no direct power but can act only through her husband. So she has to get him to move, to do, and I think it is her need to act (a need which takes her beyond all other considerations) which I most enjoyed playing in her. It's like standing on top of a mountain or an abyss and instead of shrinking or thinking 'Ahh, it's horrifying!', thinking 'We could jump!' – knowing it would bring your own destruction, but feeling that wonderful resplendence, like James Cagney at the end of *Public Enemy*, crying, 'Look, I'm on top of the world, Ma!' in exhilaration, as he is shot and the gas tank explodes under him. I was so struck by one passage in Sanders that I transcribed it:

> There is a soul of goodness at the heart of evil itself, not because of it or in relation to it, at the core of it, as is manifested by Lady Macbeth. It is as if Shakespeare, who knew that the meek must and do inherit the earth, also saw from a different point of view, Nietzschean or Lawrencian, what a disaster it would be for the earth if they did; and preserved at the very core of his conception of evil is an awareness of dynamism and power.[1]

We do need people like Lady Macbeth, driving onwards to darkness but finding a kind of energizing truth to herself as she does so. But my main approach was: keep her vulnerable, keep her volatile. I love volatility, and it can be a very useful quality to bring to a character who may otherwise seem predetermined or monumental.

Now, of course, it's not entirely a matter of how just one performer in the cast sees the role. Lady Macbeth appears in very few scenes, and nearly all of them are with her husband: much of the work for any actors playing Lady Macbeth and Macbeth has to go into producing a credible portrait of what is certainly the most compellingly depicted marriage in the whole of Shakespeare. So from early on I needed to work closely with our Macbeth, Greg Hicks, on how these two behaved together, on what sort of story lay behind their relationship, on who they were and had hitherto been as a couple. Here there were complications. Dominic Cooke, our director (whom I ultimately found very helpful) spent a lot of rehearsal time doing improvisations and research and all sorts of other exercises, until long after the point at which most of the cast, especially Greg, were desperate to just get on with doing the play, to turn to Shakespeare's text and the immediate local business of making it work. It was weeks before we actually got to grips with the play, which I think was a mistake: *Macbeth* was due to be the first production to open in the RSC's whole season of tragedies, and that put even more pressure on us, an even more anxious sense that the rehearsal process was not getting to the point quickly enough.

[1] Wilbur Sanders, 'An Unknown Fear: *The Tragedie of Macbeth*', in *The Dramatist and the Received Idea* (Cambridge, 1968), pp. 253–307: 295.

It may be the shortest of the tragedies, but that doesn't mean you don't need all the time for working on it that you can get! So Greg and I did not spend as much rehearsal time on our scenes together as we would have liked, which was frustrating, and, furthermore, I soon sensed that he started from a very different idea about the relationship from the one I was forming. As far as Greg was concerned – and it's a fair enough perspective for someone playing the title role in *Macbeth*! – the play was primarily about what happened to and in Macbeth, and he really just wanted his Lady Macbeth to be straightforwardly evil, a sort of external stimulus that he could brood about. I think he assumed I would just play her as an awful bad creature, so that he could get on with being a fascinating, vulnerable, flawed human being. So there was a slight contretemps when he discovered that I was not going to play her just as an evil queen, with him saying we could not both be sensitive and complicated and me assuring him we could and, moreover, that the text demanded it. But very soon, as we got to grips with actually playing the scenes together, we found our way through. I am very glad, though, that the production ran for as long as it did – we finished in London almost a year after we opened in Stratford – because we went on learning how to play to and around one another throughout the run. The relationship between Lady Macbeth and Macbeth grew. They still wound up alienated and dying at every performance, of course, but that's tragedy for you.

The picture of this marriage that the play presents is so rich but so short that you do have to decide what sort of shared history your performances are going to suggest. We decided that we had been married at least ten years, and – in response to the famous 'How many children had Lady Macbeth?' question, that is supposed to be so disreputable but that performers do actually have to answer for themselves and for their audiences – that there had been a child, who had died. I don't think you need to go into more specifics than that – too much novelizing and implied detail can just get in the way – but clearly they had briefly been parents, but that trajectory had failed for them, the child was dead, and things had not improved between them since. The couple depicted in the text clearly do love each other, and they both understand that they need each other equally too: he needs her support and approval, and she needs him because in this world she cannot do or achieve anything except through a man. Now that motherhood is closed to her – despite Macbeth's flattering

'Bring forth men children only . . .' (1.7.72–4), we did not think they really believed there were any further children to come, for whatever reason – she is utterly thwarted, she depends on him to express herself. She loves him, and is proud of him, in almost a motherly way: but she does see what she terms his weakness, which is his imagination, his inwardness. She does not have that: she is a sensual, immediate, Renaissance creature who does not have a thought separate from acting upon it. That's her tragedy – she does not think enough, whereas his is the opposite. And it is tragic, too, that she loses that spontaneous, unthinking immediacy: by the time we reach the sleepwalking scene, she has split apart, she turns out to have had a moral imagination all along, somewhere repressed underneath, and it is irrupting through her nightmares in ways she does not understand and cannot control.

She turns out to be inhabited, in fact, by one of the themes of this play which any performer in one of the lead roles is especially conscious of: time. The play not only manipulates our sense of how fast time is passing, and depicts a couple trying and desperately failing to have a stake in the future, but keeps talking about time – so much so that between them Macbeth and Lady Macbeth say the word 'time' something like forty-four times. There is a rhythm of reminders of time right through the text: the play's very first word is that urgent 'When . .?' from the first witch, 'When shall we three meet again?' In our production, I wanted the first glimpse of Lady Macbeth to be a tiny snapshot of a moment just before the starting gun, just before this chain of events starts racing inevitably forwards: so 1.5 began with a little domestic pause, with Lady Macbeth sitting eating a bowl of soup in the gap between having first read his letter about the witches' prophecy and then rereading the bulk of it aloud, 'They met me in the day of success . . .' (1.5.1–13). It is a glimpse of a woman unwillingly becalmed, sitting there as if before the letter had even arrived, thinking, 'When is something going to happen? When am I going to be able to live?' (Perhaps this is where she is closest to Hedda Gabler.) And as she reads the letter again, and the possibilities it opens up occur violently to her, that something does start to happen. She is obsessed with time: she feels time is running out, she cannot bear to miss any opportunity, and though she and her husband love each other she senses that something is missing and perhaps feels that time is running out for the marriage too. They have had great passion in the past, but what we first see in Lady Macbeth is frustration. Then suddenly, as she reads the letter, it is as if the possibility of renewing their passion is sparked by this overmastering idea of killing Duncan together. She is like a gambler, with this sudden sense of one great reckless throw to be made. From the moment the letter comes to the moment the murder is done, is one great arc, her commitment to it so intense that for her it could all take place in a single time-stopping second. The first thing she says when he arrives is: 'Thy letters have transported me beyond / This ignorant present, and I feel now / The future in the instant' (1.5.55–7). I found that a real key. The future in the instant: she wants to make time stop. The irony is that in an instant everything does change: in the instant it takes to kill Duncan, she is done for, and she and her husband become a couple not with a future but with a terrible past which they cannot escape. She cannot stop time but can only destroy herself: from the murder onwards she is in an absolute spiral to her own offstage suicide.

There is a profound moment as she begins to see this in 2.2, when she takes the daggers from Macbeth and carries them back to Duncan's chamber to incriminate the grooms. In the gap between her exit at 2.2.54 and her re-entrance at 2.2.61, she has encountered real blood, a real murdered body, a slaughterhouse: up until then, the murder has been an imaginary means to an end, something pictured as the momentary gateway to a new, fuller life, but now it is real, continuously real, and she and Macbeth have to start living in a present in which they have done it and they always will have done it. This is where her trauma begins, during that short absence from the stage. I don't know that she consciously recognizes this at the time, but she will spend much of the rest of her role recognizing it in retrospect. The way I played that transformed return from seeing Duncan's body in our production was that I came back out with blood on my hands, while Greg was downstage looking at his own at the close of 'Will all great Neptune's ocean wash this blood / Clean from my hand? No, this my hand will rather / The multitudinous seas incarnadine, / Making the green one red' (2.2.58–61). When I first re-entered I had the same total self-absorption in my bloodstained hands, as if he was speaking and thinking what we were each going through separately and in isolation. It was only when I then looked up and saw him that I had to snap out of it and resume my usual role, shaming him into getting on with how we had planned to manage the aftermath of the killing ('My hands are of your colour, but I shame / To wear a heart so white', 62–3). But it is clear from what Lady Macbeth says (and does!) in the sleepwalking scene that her experience of the scene of the crime has gone very deep; there is a profound sea-change in her from that moment. Something in her very being stops, completely caught.

Because she is more practical than Macbeth, however, she is not going to stop and have a soliloquy about it, she has to get on with doing things: and there I think she is incredibly brave, to keep herself actively going through with their plan when all the time she is finding herself not in the enriched, enlarged life she had envisaged but only among ever-diminishing returns. The next time we really hear her say anything at all is after the coronation. She has three lines after Macduff has discovered the body, when she has to convince the whole bereaved household of her innocence, resorting to her faint at 2.3.118; then one little remark at what we played as the reception following the Macbeths' coronation, 3.1, where we see her just being polite to Banquo (3.1.11–13); but the next time we actually hear her say anything substantive is a tiny, terrible little soliloquy after all the guests have gone: 'Naught's had, all's spent, / Where our desire is got without content...' (3.2.6–9). So she is in despair already, by then. She doesn't say she is sorry, mind; she never says she wishes she had never done it (Bradley has a nice phrase about her being too great to repent, which I liked); and she does not face Macbeth with her feelings of emptiness and hopelessness at all; but there is a deep sense of regret and a profound sadness. What makes her a woman you can still love (and the only way I can play a part is not just to like or understand the character but to love them, in order to be them) is the way she does not buckle or go under. She has, it turns out, sacrificed her soul in the hope of making her husband happy and making their relationship work, but she somehow manages to go on telling him that everything is going to be fine. He knows otherwise, in himself, but it is not something she will ever admit to him. She would rather die first – and she does. It is precisely because she never allows herself to express any of this, save in that tiny rhyming soliloquy, that she finally endures the breakdown we see in the sleepwalking scene.

That is what makes that moment in the previous scene, when Macbeth dismisses her so that he can be cloistered with the murderers (at 3.1.43–5), so awful: she has put herself in hell for this man, and suddenly he apparently cannot face being alone with her. I played it as much like a physical shock as I could, as if he had literally slapped her in the face. *Just as we've got what we both wanted, what we both planned and fought for, he's cutting me out!* It echoes for me that earlier moment in 1.7, when Macbeth says he has decided against going through with the murder: her 'Was the hope drunk . . .?' (1.7.35–44) to me is not just a taunt about his masculinity, but expresses a real sense of terrible betrayal that he is unilaterally trying to opt out of their joint project. (That is why she then brings out what is to her the worst possible thing she can imagine, the idea of deliberately killing the baby she has suckled, 1.7.54–59.) It is unendurable to her that he should reject her, whether out of fear, as in 1.7, or out of what the audience know is his desire to take on the next burden of guilt alone. Given the choice, of course, she would much rather share that burden: she feels as betrayed as if he were having an affair, struck dumb with shock, and at this point in the play it makes her more desperately vulnerable rather than tougher. The more remote and introverted he becomes, the more she seems to need to placate and reassure him; the darker their now increasingly disjointed lives seem, the more pathetically she struggles to pretend everything will be fine. But by the end of the banquet scene, 3.4, they are so isolated that in our production they could not even touch one another. They both know that his outburst about Banquo's ghost in front of the court constitutes completely blowing it, but there is nothing they can do: they are both exhausted by their demons. For his: 'It will have blood, they say. Blood will have blood . . .' (3.4.121–5), we were both slumped, almost unseeing, immobile, apart, and we stayed pretty much numb throughout the dialogue that follows. She still needs him, but she is exhausted; he is less human, more remote. Almost at the end of the scene, as we sat opposite each other at a table, she makes the last of her by now collapsing bids to reassure him, 'You lack the season of all natures, sleep' (3, 4, 140). On that line I put my hand out across the table towards him. Macbeth just looked blankly at my hand, and then responded to this tender gesture only with one last macho swagger, as if trying to get her to bed by posing as the ruthless, invulnerable tough guy that by now we know he isn't: 'Come, we'll to sleep. My strange and self abuse / Is the initiate fear that wants hard use' (3.4.141–2). He came to me, as if to kiss me savagely as a prelude to taking me off to bed: but it is no good, even heartless sex has failed them, he sagged before we had even touched. It was like two puppets that had had their strings cut: and on the next line, the last of the scene ('We are yet but young in deed'), he just walked off alone, leaving her desolate. And Macbeth and Lady Macbeth never see each other again in the play, and the audience never see her again until the sleepwalking scene. It was funny, we had not rehearsed playing it that way at all, we just did it in one of the previews, and it made perfect sense.

It provided the perfect lead, this moment, towards the sleepwalking scene. That is, of course, a real test for a Lady Macbeth – a surprisingly short scene on the page, barely sixty lines of prose during which Lady Macbeth has only six short speeches, but in many ways it is *the* scene of the role, the terrible place we see her journey has brought her to, from being so apparently clear-sighted at the beginning to having her eyes wide open but being able to see only her inner demons. The important thing, I think, is not to play a generalized sense of guilty madness, but to show exactly what she is doing and imagining from one moment to the next, registering each perception as fully and clearly as possible. For me, the 'One, two' of 'One, two, – why, then 'tis time to do't' (5.1.33–4), for example, is the remembered ticking of a clock before the killing of Duncan; everything in the sleepwalking scene is very specific, a weird, slightly off-kilter rerun of that murder. So the sleepwalking scene informed, retrospectively, how I played the murder: this is a picture of someone endlessly re-enacting a trauma, in this case that traumatic discovery of herself as a murderess, with blood on her hands, fetching those daggers from the room containing Duncan's body. But what makes Shakespeare so extraordinary is his ability to show us, at the same time, that Lady Macbeth is reliving these events with a difference. 'Wash your hands, put on your nightgown, look not so pale' (59–60): there is a terrible, sad compassion in those words, quite different from the purposeful nagging she actually voiced at the time, as though every time Lady Macbeth re-enacts these events in her head she realizes more fully how awful they are and just how much they have cost. Even the terrible thought of their subsequent crimes cannot stop this one coming back ('The Thane of Fife had a wife. Where is she now? What, will these hands ne'er be clean?', 40–1). And we are told that this is just a tiny glimpse of one incident of sleepwalking out of perhaps hundreds, with Lady Macbeth sliding ever further into this state of intolerable conscience. It is actually a very simple scene: here is a woman who has so much been a creature of fact, of action, of the material world, who is now being overwhelmed by her repressed horror at what she has done through reliving it as fact. That is what is so awful, the fact that she is actually reliving the smell of the blood, the feeling of it on her skin, the sound of the bell, the discovery of how much blood the old man had in him, the knocking at the gate. Simple, sensuous, tactile things; there is a wonderful rightness that it should be these that finally drive her into insanity, and thence to death. The text does not specify how she kills herself – in the last speech of the play, Malcolm says he hears that she 'by self and violent hands / Took off her life' (5.11.36–7) – but I have always imagined she finally repeated the crime on herself, stabbing herself with a dagger as if re-enacting it one last time but in a sort of poetic justice.

I had the good fortune to be playing Lady Macbeth at the same time as playing another tragic Shakespearean queen, Gertrude, and it is interesting to reflect that Gertrude in many ways has much of what Lady Macbeth seems to need: a secure position as queen, a grown-up son, a husband who is a successful regicide who does not blab about seeing ghosts . . . In a funny way, Gertrude is the more political of the two, despite Lady Macbeth's reputation as a figure of ambition or megalomania: Lady Macbeth never talks about Scotland, but helps make her husband king of it primarily for reasons to do with their marriage. It is Gertrude whose marriages look more like political career moves, even though she has not had to take part in a murder to secure her position, and compared to Lady Macbeth she seems at first more introspective, more passive, and infinitely less vital – she is not driven by need. Of course, she does not know that Claudius has killed her first husband until Hamlet tells her, and it is only from there onwards that she becomes vitally engaged with the people around her, to the extent, in our production, of sacrificing herself to try to save her son and the kingdom. If Old Hamlet had not been king, would Gertrude have urged him to make himself lord of Denmark by whatever means presented themselves? And could Lady Macbeth ever have become settled and complacent, had she achieved what Gertrude has had bestowed upon her before *Hamlet* begins? It is very hard to imagine so!

8 'Why should I play the Roman fool . . . ?' (5.10.1): Simon Russell Beale
as Macbeth.

Macbeth

SIMON RUSSELL BEALE

Simon Russell Beale, CBE, played the title role in John Caird's production of *Macbeth* at the Almeida theatre in 2005. He is an Associate Artist of the National Theatre as well as an Associate Actor of the Royal Shakespeare Company. His Shakespearean roles at the RSC have included Edgar, Ariel, Richard III and Thersites, and at the National he has played Iago (for which he was nominated for an Olivier Award) and Hamlet (for which he won an Evening Standard Award). He played Malvolio and Uncle Vanya at the Donmar Warehouse in 2002–3, winning an Olivier Award for the latter. Other major stage roles have included Mosca, Edward II, Tom Stoppard's Guildenstern and Ibsen's Oswald: on the screen he has played Widmerpool in *A Dance to the Music of Time* and the Second Gravedigger in Kenneth Branagh's *Hamlet*.

Halfway through his story, having completed his preparations for the murder of Banquo and within his wife's hearing, Macbeth says this:

> Light thickens, and the crow
> Makes wing to th'rooky wood.
> Good things of day begin to droop and drowse,
> Whiles night's black agents to their preys do rouse.
> Thou marvell'st at my words. . . .

> (3.2.51–5)

Lady Macbeth is uncharacteristically dumbstruck. Her husband is employing a voice that she has never heard him use before. One would expect darkness, of course, but this passage is also lyrical, loving, almost comforting. Macbeth is weaving a spell that is self-protective and excluding. He places himself in a landscape where the course of events is predictable and inevitable – a landscape in which his wife can no longer play a part.

During the first rehearsal of this scene (but not in my previous readings of the play, when the significance of this passage somehow slipped by me), it occurred to me that, despite their growing estrangement, Lady Macbeth's astonishment is shared by her husband. He takes himself by surprise and is oddly delighted. His ease with a new language and with the power of a flowing poetic imagination is a thrilling experience for him. The audience has seen hints of this in his earlier soliloquies, but it is in this scene that he allows himself for the first time to talk in this way to another human being. I suppose that at least part of Macbeth's intention is to communicate something to the person closest to him, but, significantly, all he succeeds in doing is to reveal that what he is now thinking and feeling is essentially incommunicable. He is beginning to shut himself into a private world, a world that is, at this point, a refuge but that will become a prison.

I found, during our work on the play, that it was Macbeth as a poet, as the creator of a new vision, rather than as a soldier or a king, that I found most intriguing and mysterious. Charting the progress of a man who redefines himself as he analyses his experience became, for me, the single most important and interesting challenge.

At the beginning of the play, self-analysis seems the furthest thing from Macbeth's mind. He enters with Banquo, his professional colleague and, perhaps, a friend, having fought and won a battle that has, in effect, thwarted an attempt to invade Scotland to overthrow Duncan, the country's present king. A moment before this, we have heard a Captain, who witnessed the fight, describe it in heroic terms, although there is no doubt that the whole affair has been hard and bloody. Macbeth might be 'Valour's minion' (1.2.19), or, as he is later described by Ross in the same scene, 'Bellona's bridegroom' (54), but he and Banquo seem intent, even in the eyes of a fan like the Captain, on creating 'another Golgotha' (1.2.40).

One would expect, after this, that the two generals would be adrenalized, perhaps triumphant. In fact, Banquo and Macbeth are, to say the least, laconic. If they feel triumph (or despair), then the expression of such feelings is minimal. Macbeth describes the day as 'foul and fair' (1.3.36), a comment that gives little away; and Banquo, not responding to this, confines himself to a practical question: 'How far is't called to Forres? . . .' (37). We see two men who have, in the course of a day's work, been through a type of hell, but who have no desire to discuss it or indulge either in self-congratulation or a mutual misery. Importantly, too, in a play where sleep (or the lack of it) plays such a prominent part, they must both be tired. From this point, of course, Macbeth never sleeps easily again.

It is important, I think, that, insofar as one can say this in the context of the military structures of the time, Banquo and Macbeth are seen to be professional soldiers. This allows, as I have already hinted, for a certain detachment in the two generals. It allows, too, for an apparent delight in the king for a job well done. But that, of course, is not the whole story. Just because nothing is said about the political implications of the generals' success does not mean that such ideas are not in the air. The difficulty lies in the fact that, since any subversive thought is unexpressed, it is also unformed. A discussion of whether or not Macbeth (or indeed, Banquo) has had thoughts of becoming king before the play begins is, in one case, irrelevant. The fact is that once the idea has been definitively expressed by the Weird Sisters, then, and only then, does it become real. On hearing the prophecies, Macbeth's heart begins to race:

> why do I yield to that suggestion
> Whose horrid image doth unfix my hair
> And make my seated heart knock at my ribs
> Against the use of nature?

(1.3.133–6)

This increased heartbeat is due as much to thought being defined and expressed as to the fear and excitement such thought, in itself, leads to. (It is interesting, though, that the thought of *murder*, not mentioned by the Weird Sisters, should be the one, the 'horrid image', that Macbeth visualizes. Perhaps this is an indication of a natural inclination, the fulfilment of which is, again, a source of excitement.)

Unspoken mistrust, fear, suspicion are there on both sides of the political divide. During rehearsal, we became interested in the possibility that any dissatisfaction in the generals' minds may be mirrored by figures at the court – especially Duncan and his two sons. That Malcolm (and, by persuasion, Donalbain) is tearful, is there for all to see, but perhaps Duncan, too, delighted though he may be that his kingdom has been saved, is unsure about Macbeth. Behind expressions of gratitude and the offer of a new title, is there a considerable anxiety? Macbeth cannot be allowed to become over-mighty, but equally he cannot be left unrewarded or under-appreciated. The fact that the general is so difficult to read, gives so little away, can only exacerbate the delicacy of any negotiation. Duncan's mistake, and this could be a sign of weakness or of virtue, is not to follow through with pre-emptive action. But then, unlike Brutus in *Julius Caesar*, who kills a man because he 'may' do the unthinkable and accept a crown, and who subsequently suffers for his being party to such a murder, perhaps Duncan considers inaction a risk worth taking.

Fear and suspicion, however, do not seem to extend to Banquo. For example, he seems, unlike his colleague, at ease with the king. Macbeth, the man of few words, can come out only with speeches that seem stiff and formulaic when at court. It is surely not accidental that, in talking to Macbeth, the king says 'I have begun to plant thee and will labour / To make thee full of growing' (1.4.28–9), but it is Banquo who, albeit in a different context, elegantly picks up the metaphor: 'There, if I grow, / The harvest is your own' (1.4.33–4) – and this after the king, in our production, has broken down in tears and hugged Banquo, a gesture of physical intimacy and affection that seems inconceivable in any conversation with Macbeth. Is there something here, in Macbeth and Banquo, similar to the relationship between Cassio and Iago in *Othello* – between a man who is easy, socially adept, ideal for promotion, and the other who is 'honest' enough, good enough at his job, but difficult, anti-social?

I had always thought, in my limited knowledge of the play, that Macbeth was popular. That, it appeared, was why he is eventually elected or chosen as king. But there is no need for anyone to *like* Macbeth. So long as he performs better than anyone else (in other words, keeps winning battles when asked to do so), then his increasing power lies solely in his abilities, and he, for his part, need play no courtly games, presenting himself with as few explanatory words as possible and letting his results speak for themselves. (In this, of course, he differs significantly from Iago who, when I played him, seemed to me to be irredeemably ordinary, both in the workplace and in his under-standing of human nature.) Macbeth's last concern is with popularity. I'm not even sure that Banquo likes him. We see familiarity, perhaps respect, in their relationship, but not necessarily affection.

In other words, Macbeth starts the play as an isolated man; and this isolation was something that, over the weeks of rehearsal, we decided to push as far as the text would allow us. For the audience, for the other characters (including, at important moments, his wife), Macbeth is an unknown, unfathomable quantity, and the tragedy of his life stems from his being unknown to, or unexplored by, himself. Circumstances, and his reaction to them, force him to begin a process of self-exploration, which (unlike Hamlet's, say), proves to be personally disastrous.

For the two actors, Macbeth's relationship with Banquo must be examined (indeed, invented) off the text and away from the principal thrust of the story. As I have said already, Shakespeare gives precious few clues as to what they may feel about each other. They have only one exchange of two short lines before the extraordinary events of the play disturb the normal rhythm of their lives and work together. Macbeth hides behind silence and, after the appearance of the Weird Sisters, a certain grim, dismissive humour. Banquo is more generous, with his words and in his thought. The three Weird Sisters (who never refer to themselves as witches and, indeed, seem to consider such a description offensive, 1.3.5ff.) were, in our production, rather grand ladies, rather than camp-following scavengers or down-and-outs. The idea that they should be impressive, perhaps even of a higher status than the two generals, came from a print in an edition of the Holinshed narrative that Shakespeare used as a source for the plays, in which the three women look like versions of Edith Sitwell. It was entirely in keeping with Banquo's sense of social ease that it was he who should feel able to talk to them when Macbeth, for whatever reasons, kept his mouth shut. And Banquo is generous in other ways; this talking to the Weird Sisters first shows a protective instinct, a concern for his partner. Later, he tries to dissuade him from any precipitate action and shows a trusting desire to talk with Macbeth about the significance of the women's prophecies. He does not shut his friend out, as Macbeth does, however uncomfortable or frightened he might feel about the promises of kingship for Macbeth and for his own descendants. Such openness of spirit is definitely not Macbeth's style.

There is another major factor which has the potential to drive the two men further apart. Inevitably, the fact that Banquo has a son (and Macbeth does not) will become a major focus for discontent – at least on Macbeth's side. There is a scene when all three of them meet – Macbeth, Banquo and Fleance – and it is a fascinating one.

It is the night of the murder and Banquo, still waiting for a promised talk with Macbeth about the Weird Sisters' words and unable to sleep, walks with his son around his host's castle. They meet Macbeth, already, unbeknown to them, well on the way to resolving the ambiguities of his situation by killing the king. He certainly, and typically, has no desire to share any of his thoughts with his erstwhile colleague. Banquo brings up the subject of the Weird Sisters, to which Macbeth replies:

> I think not of them;
> Yet, when we can entreat an hour to serve,
> We would spend it in some words upon that business
> If you would grant the time.

(2.1.20–3)

It is as if Macbeth knows that the first small lie – that he has not been thinking of the prophecies – is unconvincing and that he has to offer something to Banquo. But is this merely a sop, a diversionary tactic, or could it be more complicated than that? Is it, in fact, for a brief moment, a genuine offer of a deal? Is Macbeth saying, with Fleance in front of him, 'I will be king and promise to acknowledge, since I have no children, your son, who could one day be king, as my heir'? After all, there are an odd couple of lines, after Banquo shows himself willing to talk, where Macbeth implies the possibility of mutual benefits: 'If you shall cleave to my consent, when 'tis, / It shall make honour for you' (24–5). In the end, I felt it was wrong, or at least less interesting, to presume that Macbeth is being simply Machiavellian, playing for time. What if, even for a short moment, he saw a way of achieving his ends with a minimum of destruction, the possibilities of the one murder being the 'be-all and the end-all'? As we know, his paranoia after the murder of Duncan will never allow this to happen and the one death leads to many others, but at this stage perhaps Macbeth is subconsciously trying to pursue a less destructive path than the one he eventually follows. Perhaps, too, there is an emotional, as well as strategic, need to include a live and healthy Fleance in his plans. There is a similarity here with Claudius in *Hamlet*. Having committed one murder and having no desire to commit another, hoping that life will return, as far as is possible, to something resembling the *status quo ante*, Claudius seems genuinely to want Hamlet as his son and heir. Or, at least, he could do. Political and personal motives may be hard to isolate, and if political and personal needs can be satisfied in the same action, or series of actions, then so much the better. Macbeth, a childless man contemplating murder and usurpation without the security of an heir, may feel something similar.

This was why, in our production of the play, Fleance suddenly appeared with his father, when, after the murder of Duncan, they plan to go riding. This appearance, a forceful reminder for Macbeth that there is unfinished personal and political business, elicited an irritated and surprised reaction from the new king: 'Goes Fleance with you?' (3.1.37). Macbeth wants, needs, to keep Fleance with him. The fact that Banquo obstinately pursues an independent course of action, even in so trivial a matter as going riding one afternoon with his son, ensures that the frightened and suspicious king has no option but a further round of murder. Because Banquo, a man who knows too much for comfort, does not play the game, has no desire to strike a bargain, he has to die.

Part of the problem in the relationship with Banquo is, needless to say, Macbeth's difficulty in communicating his thoughts and desires with any real clarity. In part because of the dangers of the situations the characters find themselves in, and in part because of Macbeth's own nature, all communication of any importance (at least at the beginning of the play) is conducted through hint and suggestion. The strange scene between Macbeth and the two men he hires to murder Banquo is a case in point, although, in this instance, Macbeth speaks too much and not too little. Suddenly, and unexpectedly, this man of few words employs a great torrent of language. There are many possible reasons for this. Perhaps Macbeth is testing the waters of his new position, enjoying the fact that people *have* to listen to him now that he is king. Perhaps he is, on the contrary, nervous about how to behave and about the request he is making. The fact that he talks so much could indicate either that he is at ease with these two men from a different world and a lower class or that he is deeply uncomfortable. The strangeness of the scene lies in the fact that, whatever the reasons for his behaviour, there is absolutely no need for him to talk so much. The two potential murderers require no real persuasion to carry out a murder and are hardly in a position to refuse the king's request. And, ironically, the mass of language serves to obfuscate rather than clarify – the king referring, as he does with his wife, to 'the business' and later to 'the dark hour', and never putting his argument forward with any clarity.

In the first scenes with Lady Macbeth, the more typical problem of Macbeth's taciturnity is in evidence. He says almost nothing, relying correctly on his wife's ability to read him. When he refers obliquely and euphemistically to 'this business' and states emphatically that he does not want to pursue it (1.7.31), Lady Macbeth attacks him furiously for his lack of resolve, despite the fact that there has as yet been no possibility for a discussion between the two about precisely what they mean to do and how they mean to do it. This might be a Shakespearean sleight of hand (in cases like these, it is argued that such things would never be noticed in performance), but, on the other hand, it might be an indication of the closeness of their relationship. There is a circularity here that is difficult to untangle. Is part of the reason that Macbeth is so uncommunicative with everybody around him the fact that he enjoys the luxury of an intense and mutually comprehending marriage? Or is the almost obsessive and exclusive relationship with his wife the result of his difficulties in the larger world – an escape and a haven, in effect?

What is unquestionably true is that Macbeth and Lady Macbeth are, in some way, locked into each other – not necessarily happily or even lovingly, but with an intensity that is potentially dangerous and destructive. This may have something to do with the vexed question of children. Although the debate about the number of children Lady Macbeth has was presented, many years ago now, as a bit of a joke, it is a subject that simply cannot be avoided or left unresolved by the two actors playing husband and wife. I suspect, too, that in Shakespeare's company (even in an environment where there were different notions of character and motive) similar questions were asked. Who and where, precisely, is the child that Lady Macbeth talks about? Emma Fielding and I, like so many people who have played the Macbeths before us, felt the need to invent a precise back-story. I suppose ours was the simplest of all the options. A child was born to the Macbeths who lived only long enough to have been suckled by Lady Macbeth and whose death was as traumatic as any such death would be for a married couple. There were no subsequent children and perhaps even their sex-life has withered under the presence of an incurable grief. Consequently, attacks on Macbeth's virility always hit home.

Lady Macbeth mentions the dead child only as a last resort. It is her final move in the argument about whether or not to kill Duncan. It is almost as if the subject has never been mentioned and is unbearably painful for her, of course, and, perhaps more surprisingly, for him. For Macbeth to watch his wife in pain is agonizing enough for him to realize that the murder of the king is, in her eyes, a gesture of love, of faith in the continuing validity of their marriage. Movingly, he responds to her grief both with an unspoken acknowledgement of his weaknesses and with a sad half-promise of more children:

> Bring forth men-children only,
> For thy undaunted mettle should compose
> Nothing but males.

> (1.7.72–4)

It is a promise that can, or will, never be honoured and they both know it, but as a declaration of love it is generously offered and silently accepted.

It is a commonplace that Lady Macbeth does not wish to consider, or simply does not see, the implications, both moral and practical, of their proposed action, and maybe it is her own pain that blinds her. There is a possibility that she sees the crown as a way of easing this pain or, like her husband, as a means of redefining herself, her role, her life. Either way, the whole adventure ends in failure, as her final breakdown shows.

Macbeth is fully aware that the murder of Duncan will in all probability lead to other crimes and to his own psychological damage, but the risk is worth taking, not only for the simple reason that he is an ambitious man, but also because in finding a new place for them in the world, he can make his wife happy and his marriage secure and fulfilling. What they both fail to foresee is that the murder of Duncan and the usurpation of the crown will, ironically, lead to the fracturing of their marriage. If the whole plan started in a need to show mutual love and dependence, then it is inevitable that, once things start to go wrong, love is replaced with mutual (though unstated) recrimination. This forces both parties to follow individual and exclusive paths and that this happens, and how it happens, seems to me to lie at the heart of the play.

Of course, they could have done nothing and still have achieved what they wanted. Macbeth's decision to force the pace, as it were, and not to wait for events to take their course, has a flavour of spiritual experiment. As I have already pointed out, his first words to the audience reveal a state of fear and excitement, a heart racing. The prophecies themselves are morally neutral (they 'cannot be ill, cannot be good'), but Macbeth, unaccountably, and unnecessarily, sees himself as having a choice between good and bad, and it is the bad that takes hold of his imagination and thrills him. He is even prepared to risk punishment in the afterlife, to 'jump the life to come', if only he can keep the present under control. Macbeth commits a crime because, like a gambler, it is risk that he finds exciting and, whether or not there is 'judgement here', in this world, an exercise of will should surely minimize its adverse effects on his own life. As part of the bargain, he is willing, or rather wants, to live only in the present, with no past (where there is a dead child), or the future (where there should be another child, an heir).

At a point towards the end of one of his greatest soliloquies, the idea of children and the idea of time coalesce in one extraordinary idea. Macbeth describes pity as 'a naked, new-born babe' (1.7.21), an image whose meaning is impossibly difficult – how, for a start, can pity be like a baby? It doesn't, in any limited way, make sense, but is nevertheless extremely powerful. In fact, its not making sense is precisely what contributes to its power. It may be unlooked for (Macbeth has long ago wiped his mind of any thought of children) and, in his surprise, he couples the idea of a baby, of a future, with the concept of pity, an emotion that combines a regret for the past, fear for the future and a desire to effect change in the present.

I suspect that Macbeth sees such a denial of past and present as both a price to pay and as a liberation, part of the prize for his daring to redefine himself. The ultimate irony of the play is that Macbeth ends as a man who is *un*defined, living from day to day, enduring a life where any action he might take has no real consequence, either good or bad. His life becomes his punishment, which is why perhaps he cannot relinquish it, fighting to the end like a bear at the stake. This absence of possibilities is something that Macbeth can simultaneously experience, analyse and express:

> Tomorrow, and tomorrow, and tomorrow
> Creeps in this petty pace from day to day
> To the last syllable of recorded time,

And all our yesterdays have lighted fools
The way to dusty death.

(5.5.18–22)

As he wished, time has collapsed, but instead of finding freedom, Macbeth has rendered his universe meaningless.

The whole of the last battle, the last beat of the play, shows Macbeth as a man now stuck helplessly between action and inaction. He both wants to fight and can't really be bothered; he both wants to live and knows that his life is worthless. This is why we decided, at this point, to present him as almost wholly inactive, waiting for the enemy, waiting for the prophecies to be fulfilled, waiting for the future to come to him. He sat, huge and immobile, in a large chair. He got up twice; once to fight, lazily and carelessly, with Young Seyton, and once when he realized that Birnam Wood was, at last, advancing on Dunsinane and that a man 'not of woman born' was likely to be close behind. He accuses others of tying him to the stake, whereas, of course, the fault (or, at least, the decision not to move) is entirely his own.

The chance of redemption, of forgiveness or of starting again on a different path has long since gone, but, oddly, there are, in Macbeth, flickers of remorse or regret. Whether or not this is evident in the reaction to the death of his wife is debatable, and although he gives a severe account of a world around him that offers not 'honour, love, obedience, troops of friends' but 'curses, not loud but deep, mouth honour, breath' (5.3.27–9), this could be read as simply accurate rather than self-pitying. But when he finally meets Macduff (the man whose wife and children he has killed) he can no longer hide from the consequences of what he has done: 'Of all men else', he says,

I have avoided thee.
But get thee back. My soul is too much charged
With blood of thine already.

(5.10.4–6)

It is here that the final twist in Macbeth's journey manifests itself. As in *Richard III* the murder of children is seen as unforgivable. Richard, whose killings in the early part of the play are feebly excused as the necessary outcome of political expediency, knows in his heart that his order to kill the princes in the Tower is deeply wrong. Even the man who commits the murders, Tyrell, knows it is wrong. Similarly, although Macbeth can persuade himself that the deaths of Duncan and Banquo are in some way necessary, there is no escaping the fact that the murder of Macduff's children is arbitary, unnecessary and cruel. But it is only now, in the last meeting between Macduff and the man who murdered his children (or, from a different perspective, Macbeth and the father of the children he has killed) that the full implications of his action impinge upon Macbeth. Does he, despite his fighting talk, finally give up? If, after all, his death is now out of his hands, the final prophecy having now come true, does Macbeth resign himself to the fact that he has to die, to stop the misery inflicted on others and the misery he himself is suffering? It seems a glaring contradiction to the idea of Macbeth as a man who does not look for death, even believes that he cannot die, but we decided that he should trick Macduff into helping him with a sort of assisted suicide. Perverse or not, this idea had the benefit of being characteristically devious (he pretended to attack Macduff, while simultaneously exposing his body to his opponent's knife) and it highlighted, too, the fact that, at this stage, Macbeth does not care whether he lives or dies. Both life and death are equally terrible. In fact, Macbeth died long ago, and whether he goes on breathing or not has become a minor detail. His tragedy is that everything, including his own death, has been drained of meaning.

King Lear

9 'Here's a night pities neither wise men nor fools' (3.2.12–13): John Normington as Lear's Fool.

Lear's Fool

JOHN NORMINGTON

John Normington played the Fool in Bill Alexander's Royal Shakespeare Company production of *King Lear* in 2004. One of the most regularly in-demand actors of his generation, he appeared in the famous John Barton–Peter Hall *Wars of the Roses* cycle for the RSC in 1965, and played Flute in Peter Hall's film of *A Midsummer Night's Dream* in 1968. For the RSC he has also appeared in *The Comedy of Errors*, *Twelfth Night*, *As You Like It*, *Love's Labour's Lost* and Ibsen's *Ghosts*. During the 1960s and 1970s he appeared in much of the most important engaged and social realist theatre produced in Britain, including the premiere of Pinter's *The Homecoming*, while his screen work has ranged from *Rollerball* to *Will Shakespeare* to *Casualty*.

The case of the fool without a name: a detective story

By John Normington

'**Y**ou have one message', the voice said. I hit playback. 'A palace official filed a "missing person's" and Bill Alexander's in charge of the investigation. He wants to see you. He needs help.' I headed over to the RSC's headquarters in Earlham Street. It was a walk up. I legged it three flights into a large reception room. A minder hid behind an *Evening Standard*. I coughed. She lowered the paper to veil level. 'What's a four-letter word for "copycat"?', she asked. She pushed her readers to the top of her head. 'Actor?', I said. 'That's five', said the mid-forties blonde. 'You here to see Bill?' I nodded. 'Follow me.' She marched me down a corridor and pointed at a door with her emery-board. 'Go right in, he's waiting for you.' I knocked. The door opened. Bill wore a look that managed to be laid-back and hassled at the same time. 'The guy's been missing for four hundred years', Bill said, 'and we don't even have a name for him.' 'A John Doe',[1] I said. 'Yes', said Bill. 'The only clue I have is this.' He handed me a copy of *King Lear* by William Shakespeare. The Penguin edition. 'The guy just disappeared. He walked into a void and vanished. Where the hell did he go?' he said. The case interested me. That was autumn 2003.

Bill was directing *King Lear* for the RSC and he was looking for a Fool. I went to see him. It wasn't a line-up, nothing like that. I'd just never worked with Bill on a case before, so this was a friendly 'glad to meet you' kind of thing. It turned out we never got around to discussing any of the finer points of the case: to be honest I don't think either of us had any clear idea what the finer points would be. 'We need a body', I said. We needed to dust for fingerprints, 'but how do you dust after four hundred years?' I said. We needed to interrogate suspects, but how do you cross-examine anyone four centuries later? They'd all be dead. So what do I do? Well, I got one tip-off. The Fool could have doubled with Cordelia – that's the king's youngest daughter. They never meet in the play so maybe . . . but wait a minute. If Robert Armin, one of Shakespeare's clowns, was playing John Doe, as most of the old guys seem to think, he'd have been forty, too old to play a young girl, so that's a red herring. (Besides, some other officers had tried pursuing that line in the past, and for me it had just never added up.) Shakespeare drops the Fool suddenly. Why? I got a call from my agent. Bill had turned the case over to me officially, and I was assigned to play the Fool in Stratford in the 2004 season. It's a great part to play, and now that I had been promoted to whip in charge of the investigation I had to find John. Thus begins my search for the body. Thus begins the detective work on The Case of the Fool Without a Name.

But of course you don't come to every new show completely new yourself, and my proper beginning in this game, which came to colour a lot of what I did in quest of John Doe, was back in the fifties. That's also when I first experienced theatre as a subdivision of detection. I was a rookie and the case was The Actress, the Bangle and the Go-Between. I earned my badge not walking a beat but working as an

---

[1] Everyman. In this case, police slang for an unidentified corpse.

assistant electrician. The actress was Patricia Pilkington, the leading lady at the Theatre Royal, Ashton-under-Lyne. She was playing Sadie Thompson this week, next week Mrs Manningham in *Gaslight*. The bangle was Sadie Thompson's. It was stolen. A search took place. Me being the dogsbody, the lowest of the low, I was the guy they sent for. 'Cock', said Patricia, 'I want you t'go up t'the market and get me a big, chunky, green bangle, mock rhinestones.' She handed me two shillings. I was fifteen, embarrassed as hell, and couldn't go back until I found that bangle. The lady on the stall wore a black turtle-neck sweater, but it was her wrist that caught my eye. A big, chunky, emerald-green bracelet hung from it. I haggled. I told her I worked in the theatre and that I could bring a lot of work her way if she'd let me have it for two shillings. 'Not for sale', she said. Then I begged. 'It's for me mam.' The emerald green was rubbing off on her wrist as she twisted the bangle and gave me a funny look. Maybe if this poor mixed-up kid wants it that desperately it would be safer just to let it go . . . She gave in, and I rushed back to the theatre in triumph with the booty – only to be told that the missing bangle had now turned up. 'Take this back and get me some earrings', instructed Miss Pilkington. The thief turned out to be Barney. Barney was an old grey dog who had the run of the theatre. The bangle must have fallen off the dressing table and Barney, determined to be of some use for once, had done a little cleaning up. Lesson one: always investigate a crime scene with proper thoroughness, checking everywhere, including the dog's basket. I got to be a familiar face on the market, what with buying and returning earrings, bracelets, you name it. That is, when I wasn't too busy in my other line of non-electrical work, namely being a Go-Between, running between Miss Pilkington and her gentlemen callers. One-night stands such as Patrick. 'Go to the stage door and find Patrick', Patricia would tell me. 'Tell him Miss Pilkington had to leave early. I won't be able to see him this evening.' Then she'd go off with someone else. For those of you who don't know, Patricia became Pat, and Pilkington became Phoenix, and Miss Pilkington became rather better known on a television programme called *Coronation Street*. I guess I owe it to Pat for turning this rookie into a sleuth.

In retrospect, maybe the smart procedure when Bill first put me on the John Doe case would have been to distribute posters all over

Stratford, or at least at the usual hang-outs – McDonald's, Marks &
Spencer's, the railway station, the Dirty Duck: 'Court Jester Missing. All Round Entertainer. Singer of Songs, Dancer, Juggler, Acro-
bat. If you can assist this inquiry, please contact the stage door of
the theatre.' What we had, in any event, as at the start of any set
of rehearsals, was a jigsaw. Every actor is a piece of the puzzle. If I
didn't solve my part of the puzzle an audience might just as well stay
home as far as I was concerned. 'If a man's brains were in's heels,
were't not in danger of kibes?' (1.5.9–10). What's kibes? The text is
full of lost meanings and oblique references, and so there was a fair
amount of preliminary spadework to put in on finding the meaning of
difficult passages. The Arden, Penguin, Everyman, First Folio, etc.,
all helped and hindered the investigation. Editors don't always agree,
and contrary views are put forward. Sometimes an editor will say,
'The true meaning of the line is now lost.' Well, thanks a lot. The
actor–detective just hit a brick wall. As for directors, I've worked with
all sorts. Some will cut passages that border on the obscure, while others feel the text must be made to communicate as written. Now I'm
concussed.

The first rehearsal begins with a read-through. This is important to
the actor–detective. True to Agatha Christie, the other witnesses are
gathered, and the evidence I get from them will supply me with clues,
vital information will slip out that I wasn't aware of. Caught-off-guard
relationships can be unmasked. With a play as violent as *Lear*, and the
circumstances of the Fool's disappearance so murky, these weren't just
witnesses, they were suspects. In my head I grilled them. 'Where were
you when John Doe vanished? Did you think his jokes were funny?
Isn't it true he criticized you in court?' By now I already had a good
grasp of the text, as I always do when I start out on a new show: with
the book in my hand I can't act or enter into the world of the play,
so the sooner I put the book down the sooner I can advance to the
next stage – finding the Fool, the human being. My character. Ralph
Richardson said, 'Look in the mirror and ask yourself, is it human?'
Am I on the right track? I gave the Fool a cockney accent. I heard
Max Miller.

I'd already played a clown or two by the time I was on the hunt for
the Fool. Manchester Library Theatre, that's where I played my first
Shakespeare. My friends Penelope Keith, Helen Frazer and Anthony

Hopkins were all in the company. I played Francis the drawer in *Henry IV*, Old Gobbo and the Prince of Aragon in *The Merchant of Venice*, Old Adam and Jacques de Bois in *As You Like It*. I was still in my twenties. In the sixties I played Quince for the RSC, and Feste at the Royal Court, then in the seventies I played Touchstone at the National. All that experience and I still didn't have the sense to realize that to play this Fool I needed to go all the way back to where I started. After a few days of Max Miller, Bill said to me, 'He's from the North – use your own background.' The voice, the core of my character, was found, and he became a Northern comic.

Growing up in the North I'd spied with my little eye many of the Northern comics of the day as they performed at the Palace, Manchester (Frank Randle, Norman Evans). The one I was drawn to was a man I worked with at close quarters, Jimmy Edmundson. I was sixteen and, building up towards Shakespearean tragedy from a fair way back, I was playing Baby Bear. My stage parents, Mama and Papa Bear, were played by a Polish trapeze act called the Amazing Lorenzos. But wait – Papa had lots of dialogue, and despite his cod Italian stage name he was Polish, in fact Polish to the point of incomprehensibility. So suddenly I was Papa Bear and, somehow, was also stage manager for the whole of *Goldilocks and the Three Bears*. Jimmy and I shared the same digs. Jimmy was the comic. He could sing, a bit. Dance, a bit. He was funny without doing anything. He told terrible jokes yet the audience laughed. On our walk to the theatre Jimmy would try out his jokes on me. He was an all-round entertainer. I could use his skills to build my Fool. So I danced, a bit. 'Fools had ne'er less grace in a year' (1.4.148–51) became a soft-shoe shuffle. Sang, a bit. The cryptic speech to Kent in the stocks, 'That sir which serves and seeks for gain' (2.2.241–58), became a sad Victorian ballad. I had a shovel and I was digging.

What did he look like? What did he wear? I got a text from the designer: 'Boots found, could be his.' I rushed over to wardrobe. Clothes everywhere. The designer frantically searching for a coat. 'Boots should be battered and old', she said, 'Try these on.' They fitted and I liked them, my toes were sticking out. I had footprints now. 'He would be dressed identical to Lear', she said, 'his clothes need to be ill-fitting as if they were the king's cast-offs. Got to find a coat for the storm scene. He'd wear an overcoat that buries him.'

Looking through some old photographs we came across Russian brothers, they'd been jesters for the last Tsars of Russia. They were wearing sashes covered in medals. The medals gave us another clue, and she incorporated them into her design. Then an overcoat was found and it buried me. A cap and bells and a jester's stick with a clown's face were her only acknowledgement to motley . . . I was dressed.

But who is he? No dental records. No fingerprints. A forensic anthropologist can do tests to determine age by bone density, but an actor, equipped not with a DB (that's a dead body) but his or her own blank, live one, has to invent, calling up imaginary witnesses from memory and imagination. I invent a history for this man, a story that will bring him to life. I am older than the king, I've decided. Under interrogation, one witness confirmed that John Doe had already been in service when the king's daughters were growing up. That Cordelia was the only daughter he had any affection for. Another said he disliked Goneril and saw through her ambition. That Regan was just as bad as Goneril, no, worse, she beat him. And another witness went so far as to confess that John, in the strictest confidence, had told him that the happiest days of his life were when those bloody sisters quit the palace and got married. The most important relationship for me playing the Fool is with the king. It was sheer luck for me that a bonding between Corin Redgrave, the king in this production, and myself was developing. In one of the previews I dried (lost my lines) in my opening scene, 1.4, and had to improvise. Corin stayed with me in my free fall until I got myself together and could continue with the scene. We stayed in our characters and he supported me and it strengthened an actors' bond between us.

As I sit in my dressing room I see the Fool in my mind's eye. He's perched in a corner looking out of the window watching the Avon flow by and rehearsing his jokes. I do my warm-up. 'Did you ever hear the one about . . . ?', he shouts. I go through my lines. 'What about the one about the parrot and the sea captain?' I've broken the text down into Units. I give the Units names. These names tell me what each section of the play is about. The storm scene I've called 'Roughing it in a storm with a mad king'. Units are broken down into smaller units, these smaller units have beats. Then we have Objectives.

The Fool's 'wants': these are his objectives. Every time someone says something in a play he wants something. The Fool wants attention from the king: *hear me, laugh at me, pity me*. I am not conscious of lines when I act, what I act is the wants underlying them. All units have objectives, and the play has a super-objective. And underneath the text is a subtext. I say A, but what I'm really saying is B. My line is: 'A fox when one has caught her, / And such a daughter, / Should sure to the slaughter, / If my cap would buy a halter' (1.4.296–9). What I mean is: 'You animal, I'd want you to hang.' Sometimes it could be something entirely different. We all do it, say one thing and it's a disguise for another. I must be aware of my subtext at all times.

I look through the case notes. We dug a long way down on this one. The earliest source for the Lear story is Geoffrey of Monmouth, a fourteenth-century monk who also wrote an important early account of the life of King Arthur. John Doe is interested in Merlin, even though he knows that King Arthur is supposed to have lived later in history than King Lear – 'This prophecy Merlin shall make, for I live before his time'(3.2.95) – it figures. Lear is mentioned in Shakespeare's favourite history book, Holinshed's *Chronicles*, and Shakespeare may himself have acted in *The True Chronicle History of King Leir and his Three Daughters* – which has a happy ending – more than ten years before he wrote *King Lear*. Ten years nerving himself up to kill Cordelia? That's what I call premeditation. One thing was clear: expecting minute evidence about exactly where and exactly when John Doe disappeared was hopeless. It was some time in Ancient Britain that was also Shakespeare's time and is also somehow ours, and it was somewhere vaguely towards Dover, but that's it. 'Drive toward Dover, friend, where thou shalt meet / Both welcome and protection', says Gloucester (3.6.49–50), but they never get there. Welcome and protection are in pretty short supply in *King Lear*. Maybe it's no wonder one of the cast disappears without trace.

Some ideas were dropped as new ones presented themselves, but that question remained: where did he go? Why does the Fool disappear after 3.5 in the Folio version, the scene in the hovel on the heath, and after scene 13 in the quarto version, the joint-stool scene in which Lear tries Goneril and Regan in their absence? (which we played – damn it, somebody has to be brought to trial in a case this upsetting!). Maybe that's a part of the puzzle that will remain unsolved. Maybe it's all inadmissible, all hearsay, and would never hold up in court – after all, most of what an actor goes on is made up, it's all in my head, like I said. But that elusiveness is what makes the Fool interesting. When Poor Tom meets the king, the Fool takes a back seat in Lear's attention. Does he just fade out like Tinkerbell because no one is laughing at him any more? Was his sole function to be funny? Or was he a man with a dark side? Was he in full possession of his faculties when he disappeared? Did he get a better job? Or did he just freeze to death out in the rain? Was he a lamb led to the slaughter, and, if so, by whom? Was he hit by a torpedo sent by person or persons unknown? Why? Who benefited? The conspiratorial elder sisters did, and because the king loved him that once made him dangerous. But by the time of the Fool's disappearance the king was not the man he was. In the very last scene of the play the king says 'And my poor fool is hanged' (5.3.281), but is he? Is that a sick man ranting? And the Fool's last line in the play turns out to be prophetic: 'And I'll go to bed at noon' (3.6.43). Is this a man recognizing that his career has come to a premature end, saying he will retire before it's time? I walked over to Poor Tom at the end of that scene and I gave him my cap and bells and walked away into the darkness.

We need to be alone now. When I enter the theatre I am an actor, but as I start to get ready I'm taken over by the Fool and only part of me still exists. When we leave the dressing room heading for the king's palace we must leave as one. Take a piece of string: it has a beginning and an end. Now reverse it and the end becomes the beginning. An actor is like a piece of string. His character's life, the part he plays, ends one night and begins the next, but the actor when he begins again must find something new, each night, to stimulate his character into life or he will die.

I said Shakespeare dropped the Fool suddenly but I was wrong. He was complete. Shakespeare said what he had to say and he was finished. A great writer knows when to finish, and *I've gone on too long*. There was a Fool before me and a Fool before him and next year there's bound to be another one. In a line-up we'll be measured on what each of us brought to the part. I felt lost after I played the Fool for my last time, but our DNAs were only a match for a limited engagement. He'll always be there waiting for us, like a chameleon, always changing, like the actors always changing, and it doesn't matter where he went. We the detectives follow in his footprints and pass on.

The file is still open.

10 'You see me here, you gods, a poor old man. . . .' (2.2.446): David
Warner as King Lear.

King Lear

DAVID WARNER

David Warner played the title role in Stephen Pimlott's production of *King Lear* at the Minerva theatre in Chichester in 2005. He was an important member of the RSC in the mid-1960s, playing a famous Hamlet for Peter Hall in 1965 and Henry VI in the Hall–Barton *Wars of the Roses* cycle of histories, among many other parts. His film roles, on which he concentrated almost exclusively for three decades, include Blifil in *Tom Jones* (1963), and the eponymous *Morgan: A Suitable Case for Treatment* (1966), as well as appearances in a wide range of other movies including *Straw Dogs, The Omen, Time Bandits, Time After Time, Star Trek VI, Titanic* and *The League of Gentlemen's Apocalypse*. His many television performances include an appearance alongside the young Bob Dylan in the tragically wiped drama, *The Madhouse on Castle Street* (1963).

Did it help or hinder us that *King Lear* has such a reputation as a Great Tragedy? Certainly the role comes with a lot of expectations. I suppose I had avoided some because to play Lear was never a major ambition of mine. I didn't come off stage from my last performance as Hamlet and start calculating that in forty years or so I should consider auditioning for Lear. Honestly, I'd be as happy playing Ray Cooney: I only agreed to play Lear instead because I knew I would get to lose my trousers. I was in the RSC in the 1960s, but I'm an actor who has played Shakespeare rather than a Shakespearean Actor, and although people would ask me from time to time over the years whether or when I would play Lear I always said I wouldn't, and meant it. It was never on the agenda. When Stephen Pimlott asked me to do it, at Chichester, I at first said no. But I saw Corin Redgrave play Lear in Stratford around then, and I used to understudy for Corin at the Royal Court, years ago. I'd seen Robert Stephens's Lear, and I'd seen Paul Scofield, in Peter Brook's production, which was wonderful and which I was absolutely devastated by (it was only

when I came really to read the play for this one that I realized in
retrospect how heavily adapted that one was, how much it was Jan
Kott's *King Lear* as much as it was Shakespeare's); and I'd seen Eric
Porter's, which I liked, and I'd seen a few others where I couldn't really
take the whole thing, for various reasons. But when I saw Corin, that
was the first time I started to think, well, I could give this a shot.
But it never occurred to me that this role was the great big Everest
of world drama. Lear only has eight scenes, after all. You hear talk
about Great Lears – Wolfit, Gielgud, Ian Holm – but they are all very
different. There is room for different actors to make their own way
in this part, and I was willing to assume, when Stephen asked me a
second time to play this role, that people saw something in me that
would make me capable of doing it. Once Stephen persuaded me
I could do it, I relaxed, and in rehearsal the atmosphere was never
that we were all tensed up to make a suicidal attempt on a sublime
peak. Of course it's a great play, but it's a great play because it works,
and lends itself to interpreters, not because it is unfathomably vast or
impossible.

When you set out to perform *King Lear*, one of the first questions
you have to address is which version you are going to play, since Shakespeare, or his early publishers, left us two – the quarto, which is longer
and includes the mock-trial scene (scene 13), and the Folio, which is
a more streamlined, revised script but which still includes some material that isn't in the quarto. I'm happy to leave the question of which
has more authority or why they differ like this to the scholars, but I do
like a say in what I have to speak, and Stephen was very keen that we
should all work together to produce our own acting text, taking our
cue from the Folio version in making it as clear and straightforward
as we could. (Though we did include the mock-trial scene.) In fact,
working with me on Lear's scenes Stephen professed himself surprised
and relieved to be dealing with an actor who actually suggested cuts
rather than resisting them – some of my most frequent questions were
'Can I lose this?' and 'Could we do without this?' – and between us
we took out a lot of what seemed like repetitions or inessentials, without I hope damaging the plot or simplifying the play's ideas (though I
did get one letter from an audience member, clearly a real *Lear* con-
noisseur, who objected to not hearing one particular speech at the
length he'd been expecting). In the early rehearsals we actually had
a lot of different editions around and made choices between them,

sometimes making small emendations of our own – in the scene with Gloucester, for example, I thought that it was just pedantic to insist on the word 'fitchew' (4.5.120) when most of our audience would much better understand 'polecat', especially when the two are metrically the same. I had some discussions with Stephen during the previews about putting a few things back in, but nothing major.

We approached the play as *King Lear*, not as *The Tragedy of King Lear*, since after all the characters at the start of the play have no idea anyone is going to wind up dead; whatever else Shakespeare writes, he didn't go in for unmitigated, preordained five-act funerals. I hadn't worked on stage for thirty years until doing Shaw's *Major Barbara* in New York in 2001, mind, so my sense of how different playing Shakespeare in the theatre is to playing anything else there isn't as highly developed as it once was. Certainly it takes more initial effort to find out what all the words mean and how all the sentences work than it does with Shaw, and you then have to think hard about how you are to make the sense immediately available to the audience without patronizing them (I was once accused of lecturing to the audience, and I wouldn't want to be vulnerable to that charge again). One thing I don't do, though, is put together a whole story in my head about what has been happening to my character before the play starts. I actually said in rehearsal to Stephen and to John Ramm, who played the Fool, 'God forbid that I should ever use the term "back-story". Let's just think of something we can do during our first scene together that will cement that relationship and show the audience how it is during the play itself.' That's when we came up with the little moment in 1.4, at the Fool's first entrance, when we had this game of both racing for the throne, and me getting there first, and then in the next scene, when all the courtiers have gone and we're left on our own, he races for it and sits on it and does something stupid. That was the only 'back-story' we had – a sense that we were accustomed to this sort of little game between ourselves. We didn't need to force anything more; the two of us got on like a house on fire in rehearsal, so those scenes came very naturally. Incidentally, that's the only time I've used the phrase 'back-story' in my entire career – that just isn't how I work. Stephen and I didn't spend any time in rehearsal speculating about what games I'd played with each of my three daughters while they were growing up – we just got on with working out how to perform what happens in the play.

Where you do have to start is with the first scene, which has the reputation of being such a difficult one to act, of being an undigested piece of fairy tale that's needed to set up the rest of the play but which is hard to make convincing emotionally – with Lear going so quickly from having Cordelia as his cherished favourite to shouting at her and banishing people. It is the hell of a pill to have to start the play off that way, and in performance I did look forward to having got it out of the way. I very much did not want to give the impression, that some Lears can give, that this was the sort of thing that happened at Lear's court all the time. As far as I was concerned, however literal-minded the love-test might have looked, it was a ceremony Lear was imposing because he genuinely did see it as the best way of avoiding trouble about the succession – so I made something of a point of announcing the rationale, 'that future strife / May be prevented – *now*' (1.1.44–5). It was important, too, to point out that Lear was himself confused to find himself so angry, so provoked by Cordelia's refusal to play along. On 'I loved her most, and thought to set my rest / On her kind nursery' (123–4) I hugged her, tenderly, as if to give the audience a glimpse of the scene Lear had thought he was going to be in, before pushing her away and reverting to anger on 'Hence, and avoid my sight!' (124).

The only note I have written in my text for that scene is right there (I don't make copious notes), and it just says, 'Gear change.' From there Lear turns to the public business of dividing Cordelia's third between Cornwall and Albany, and putting in his clause about keeping a hundred knights, which is basically exposition: it's almost as though Shakespeare had already written the later scenes depicting the rows with Goneril and Regan about the size of Lear's retinue, and had thought that he had better put some information about that side of things into the first scene to prepare his audience for it in advance. I knew from reading scholars that there is supposed to be a problem about what the 'coronet' is that Lear tells Cornwall and Albany to part between them (at 138), but it didn't seem to me to be much of a problem – Cordelia was wearing a circlet, and I snatched it off her head and threw it to them. How or if they were going physically to divide it could be their problem, and it wasn't as if the scene required it to be done then and there. It is a difficult scene, though, in terms of the amount of sheer information that it has to put over, even just in terms of showing what so many characters are called.

Even the characters who aren't going to be important in the rest of the play need to be distinguished. Burgundy, for example, whom Lear addresses first and very pointedly with the news that he has now disowned Cordelia, has clearly been the favoured suitor over France. In our reading it was a real budding relationship that was being broken between them, as Burgundy's regret at having to favour politics and diplomacy over courtship showed (he really was sorry to leave her at 246–7, and she really was upset but compassionate about it, rather than just morally smug, as she can seem, in her response at 247–9), while France was still almost a stranger to her. Had Lear allowed Cordelia her own choice between them, had he favoured Burgundy because he had got wind of the fact that she did? There aren't real answers to such questions; you just have to go with the piece.

From there we next see Lear coming in from hunting – in our production, from a central entrance, with a great carcase of a stag hanging up behind him. Stephen wanted the carcase, which I fear upstaged us all a bit, but there you are – this was almost a studio production, that entrance has to be big somehow, and we didn't have the budget for a hundred knights, just three lads who doubled and tripled and even quadrupled over the course of the play (so that a majority of my entourage consisted of France and Burgundy in different clothes). It would have been nice to have the din of a whole private army coming in from the chase, but we did what we could. When I came in, for example, I wanted to get washed, and did so in a metal bowl of cold water, which I realized in rehearsal could also double as an impromptu gong if I bashed it with a stick while calling for dinner. (If the props people had given us a wooden bowl, the scene would have turned out a lot quieter.) In a small space every prop has to earn its keep, and this one did. I was very glad to be doing Lear in the Minerva, though, rather than in a bigger theatre, because it let us off a lot of what can come over as straining after effect – I wasn't going to have to shout my head right off in the storm, and I wasn't going to have to hang onto the curtain at the end like Wolfit to remind the audience of what a superhuman physical effort it had all been. The great thing about playing this role in the Minerva was that it was always intimate, you could just act out the story right before the audience's eyes; it was a little like doing TV or film, and everything we did could be in close-up.

I'm not an actor who feels obliged to love every character he plays – I've done too many villains for that, apart from anything else – but I didn't feel that my Lear was a monster. He acts atrociously at the start of the play, it's true, but he pays for it and he realizes it, and it was important to us that the audience should see what loyalty and love and friendship he has evidently inspired in a good many of the people around him. He isn't Father Christmas, but he isn't just an evil tyrant either; if he'd habitually gone on the way he does in the first scene, which surprises everyone, the characters we nicknamed the 'white hats' – Kent, the Fool, Cordelia – wouldn't be so fond of him. The Fool, clearly, genuinely likes him; Kent likes him, and feels he can speak out in 1.1, and still respects him even after the banishment that follows; that wouldn't have been possible if Lear had been a really awful person. (We never really discussed this in rehearsal, we didn't need to; everyone in the cast just sensed that there was someone in there behind the curses who was actually likable, charming despite having been turned by kingship into this silly old fool.) He's stupid, partly because he has only ever been a king, as he comes to recognize, but I don't think there's any suggestion in the text that before these events he has ever abused his power. It's the kids who put people in the stocks, it's the kids who put people's eyes out. Lear isn't like that. For example, the only time he ever has a confrontation with a commoner is his run-in with Oswald, and what does he do with him? He just says, 'Call the clotpoll back' (1.4.46). He doesn't say, 'Clap him in irons.' When Oswald does come back, Lear 'strikes' him (on the bottom with the handle of a riding crop, in our production), and Lear laughs when the disguised Kent then trips him up, but he doesn't have him executed; that just isn't how things are in Lear's regime. The clue is that line, 'Call the clotpoll back': it's mildly rude, but in such a way that assumes a norm that isn't rude at all, and seen in comparison with the things we soon see Regan and Cornwall and Goneril getting up to it's hardly tyranny.

The main thing Lear is experiencing throughout the first third of the play, I think, is sheer bafflement, rather than the vindictive exercise of unlimited power: bafflement that other people are behaving so badly, bafflement that his own actions are producing such unanticipated and disorienting consequences. That bafflement starts, and turns into anger, in the first scene, when Cordelia says, 'Nothing' (1.1.87): nobody has ever said anything like that to him before, and he can't understand it. I had my back to the central section of the audience at that point (we had the Minerva set up with a more or less square stage, surrounded on three sides), so for many of the spectators I was communicating my response mainly with my shoulders, but I hope it was clear that Lear had never heard that sort of direct refusal before. From then on, he's finding himself in a universe he no longer quite recognizes, confused, with one thing happening on top of another and no familiar strategies left for coping with any of them; and in this bewildered and alarmed state he will indeed lash out and curse people, and tell them to go, and all those other terrible things. He just has no experience of having to deal with all this. That's what his lines told me, as I started to rehearse the part, at any rate. It seemed vital to me to show that Cordelia's 'Nothing' is the most extraordinary, world-shattering thing Lear has ever heard, and how does he deal with it? He goes ballistic. Shakespeare underlines this, too, he replays it for us in a more comic key when Kent makes the same mistake when he flies off the handle at Oswald while he's in disguise in 2.2 – he isn't used to being anything other than an earl, he can't believe he doesn't get more respect from this steward, and he fails to realize that he can't have a full-blown go at him now in front of Cornwall without winding up in the stocks.

There's a sort of mythology that goes with *King Lear* that our production didn't want anything to do with, a sense that the play either is or should be a complete quasi-religious ordeal for everyone involved. I've seen productions where the interval doesn't come until the end of Act 3, after the blinding of Gloucester, and that really is too late. Stephen and I started talking about where to place our interval about half-way through the rehearsal process, after a run-through. I cast my mind back to when I played Hamlet, when I think we really did place the interval too late – not from the point of view of the actors so much as from that of the audience. You do have to think of the spectators as well as the production, and, no matter how brilliant and moving you may be, after a certain point they'll be looking at their watches and noticing that their bottoms have gone numb. I wouldn't have been comfortable at all playing in a *King Lear* that didn't let the audience stretch or breathe until after the blinding. People are liable to come in anyway thinking, 'Oh, *King Lear*, we're in for a heavy, heavy evening', and if you then confine them for a two-hours-plus first half . . . give me a break! So what we did was have two intervals, with the first immediately after Lear has left Goneril's house, at the end of the first act: this gave 'O, let me not be mad, not mad, sweet heaven!' (1.5.45) a chance to sink in. The second one then came where the sole one often does, after the blinding. This neatly and usefully divides the play into the opening, the storm, and the endgame. I think it helps make the movement of the play clearer too – from Lear's immersion in his own anger, to his going beyond that through noticing the needs of others in the storm, especially through the shock of the encounter with the poor, naked wretch Poor Tom, to the play getting beyond even that as Lear goes mad and the perspective broadens still further. A lot of people have said that the evening zipped by, even with the extra time taken up by the additional interval, and that this division of the play really helped them understand it: one of the reviewers didn't like it, and nor did one of my friends, but on the whole I think it was a very good idea.

This meant that the middle part of the play began with Lear arriving outside Gloucester's place in pursuit of Regan in 2.2, and finding the disguised Kent in the stocks, and here we used another multi-purpose prop. The design of our production set the play in no specific period – which seems to me very faithful to the way this script is written – with many members of the cast, including Lear, in modern, black leather coats, worn inside-out just to make them slightly unfamiliar – and on arriving I produced a whisky flask, a little hip flask, and poured some out into the little metal cup and gave myself an eye-bath with it. This again, I hope, served a number of purposes: practically, it underlined the fact that Lear has just had a long hard journey in the saddle along all those dusty roads, and, furthermore, it explained why Lear didn't get angry more quickly on seeing his servant in the stocks. At first, while the Fool went across and commented on what he calls Kent's 'wooden nether-stocks' (2.2.193), I couldn't see clearly what was going on, couldn't see that he was undergoing this painful and demeaning punishment at all, so that what we'd produced as a useful piece of business also chimed with the whole play's interest in seeing, both literal and metaphorical.

I suppose another part of the reputation the role of Lear has is as a 'mad' part, but he is only really mad, if he is, in one of his scenes, the dialogue with Gloucester near Dover. I found that scene, 4.5, one of the hardest to play, that and the opening. I didn't approach it as a 'mad scene' – it isn't that in the same way that, say, Ophelia's scene with the flowers is a mad scene – and Stephen's first note to me about it was that for at least the first part of the dialogue with Gloucester this is as happy as we've ever seen Lear up to now. It's the way he moves between ideas that is fairly batty, and that's what makes it tricky to act: much of the scene is really a monologue by Lear, with only a few interjections by Gloucester, and you have to concentrate on the sense of each of the moments within Lear's speech rather than following a logical line right through it. I tried not to play it as mad, as a simulation of clinical insanity, but just as a man who is saying lots of things that just happen to be spilling out all at once in no obvious order, some lucid, some strange. (This was the only scene in which I changed a line we left in, incidentally, to help clarify one of those points, and that only by transposition: I made it 'To't luxury, pell-mell, / For Gloucester's bastard son . . .' and then 'Let copulation thrive, / For I lack soldiers', 111–13, 114–15, just because I thought that having 'Let copulation thrive' there made it clearer that Lear wanted all this indiscriminate sex so that it would procreate him a new army.) I didn't think of it as a mad scene; if anything, in my head I called it the poppy scene, because the designer, Alison Chitty, had placed a few poppies downstage, just for a suggestion of the Kentish meadows. That was a lovely surprise, late in rehearsal, and I picked just one of them, and held it up against my temple on 'I am cut to th'brains' (189), as if to suggest blood. (I resisted the temptation to do more with it, such as holding it up to one eye as if to imitate the blinded Gloucester; mustn't overuse a single prop like that.) It was beautifully simple, that design, with the stage and the costumes usually in bleached colours so that this little flash of red inevitably recalled the blood left on the floor at the end of the blinding scene before the second interval.

After that, it's another gear-change, for the recognition scene with Cordelia, 4.6. In rehearsal Stephen – who is a splendidly undictatorial director, who having cast the people he wants then trusts them to come up with ideas that would work for them – always said he just wanted us to surprise him, and we came up with another vivid close-focus detail here, in a scene which can risk being vague and sentimental. I was wheeled on in a hospital bed for this scene, and it occurred to me that on Lear's 'If you have poison for me, I will drink it' (65) perhaps there might be an actual glass or cup of something to prompt that line. What we had, in the midst of Cordelia's managing to convince Lear that it really is her, was the doctor, at her signal, passing her father a cup of wine, to help revive him. So that was something I could grab, something which could give me the idea about her possibly wanting to poison me, given how she has been treated:

> If you have poison for me, I will drink it.
> I know you do not love me; for your sisters
> Have, as I do remember, done me wrong.
> You have some cause, they have not.

> (4.6.66–8)

Cordelia then says, 'No cause, no cause', and the marvellous thing was that in rehearsal it then came to me that Lear's next line is 'Am I in France?' – so if I took a sip of the suspected poison after 'You have some cause, they have not', I could then look up, puzzled, slightly pleased, reviving, much more in command of the situation, and ask 'Am I in France?' because I'd just recognized a mouthful of decent claret. It's intricate and mildly funny and if anything makes the dialogue more real and more poignant. It humanized that situation: this wasn't a Tragedy, something grandiose and ritual, but a depiction of human beings like the audience occupying the same world as them. If you can find illuminating pieces of business like that, so much the better. Those things just came in rehearsal, and they were welcome – there's nothing sacrosanct about Shakespeare that suggests it's sacrilege to make intelligent use of props. It was so perfectly logical for Lear to be offered the drink by the doctor and say it must be poison – and it even ties up with that awful little joke of Goneril's in the last scene, when she refers to the poison she has given Regan as medicine (5.3.90).

Strangely, I found dying easier than rambling. Once I had discovered that I really could carry on our Cordelia, Kay Curram, while howling, the last scene just came. It had always seemed to me that Lear ought to die on his knees – right at the start of the play, in his first proper speech, he talks about crawling towards death (1.1.41), so it seemed only logical that that's how he should go. By now, through my body language, I was playing Lear as over eighty, though I had started him off at my own age, in his sixties (I felt he aged a good decade just within that first scene, as hints of stiffness and a stoop may have suggested even to spectators I had my back to): it seems to me that he ages very much over the action of the play, and you can do that in Shakespeare, where time-schemes are never single or literal. (Corin, I noticed, cut the line in which Lear describes himself as 'Fourscore and upwards', 5.1.54, but that seemed unneccesary to me; the play says he's over eighty, by then anyway, and you may as well go for it.) I carried Cordelia on, myself wearing a sort of white robe, and laid her out in the middle of the acting area, and knelt over her, desperately solicitous, still not quite giving up on the idea that she might revive; and late in rehearsal I hit upon the idea of taking off my robe and putting it on her as a coverlet, which I was pleased with – it seemed to point out how appalled he was that she felt so cold, to repeat the simple physical compassion he had shown to the Fool in the storm, and to repeat that stripping away of externals too. (We talked in rehearsal, as people always do, about what Lear was thinking or imagining through his last speeches – whether 'And my poor fool is hanged', 5.3.281, referred to the Fool or to Cordelia – we thought the Fool really had been hanged, offstage, though I'm not sure it makes much difference to how you hear that line.) Shown the bodies of the other sisters, I just walked mechanically around, picking familiar small items from their clothes as if looting after a battle (Lear clearly does know all about warfare from experience, as we gather from the way he talks about his falchion, 5.3.251.) I broke up 'Look, her lips' (5.3.286) into 'Look' (looking forwards, out front) and 'Her lips' (looking down at Cordelia, convinced she is speaking, bending down to listen, as if she were asking me to pick her up, to carry her somewhere). So then at the end of Lear's last speech, on 'Look there, look there' (5.3.286), I was indicating not Cordelia, but somewhere offstage, beyond the audience, as if Lear thought there might still be somewhere where he might find help, where everything might be all right, and on my knees I tried to lift Cordelia up; and tried again; and couldn't; and that's what caused the heart attack that left me collapsed across her body. Again, this seemed perfectly logical in terms of the lines; there has to be some actual cause of death, and that was it.

Our approach throughout was to treat *King Lear* just as if it were a modern play (albeit an unusually good one), and when audiences told us that they had been surprised at how clearly and directly it had spoken to them, just like a modern play, we were very pleased. The overwhelming aim was clarity: to make the argument of the play, both its narrative and its ideas, completely clear to an audience who didn't know the play (and indeed to one who did), without talking down to them at all. I was especially committed to this approach because I was brought up being taken to Stratford and not understanding a word – and a lot of that was because of productions and performances that took for granted the 'eliteness' of Shakespeare, that felt Shakespeare was only for a chosen few. As I said earlier, I wouldn't consider myself as primarily a 'Shakespearean' actor – I was in a lot of Shakespeare productions at one time when I was younger, admittedly, a couple of them important ones – but when doing Shakespeare my basic priority has always been to make it clear to the audience what is going on. If you do that properly in *King Lear*, they cry. And it's only right that they should. If we definitely achieved that at Chichester, then at least part of my ego is well satisfied.

Index